YOU'LL NEVER GUESS THE END

BARBARA WERSBA
YOU'LL NEVER GUESS THE END

A Charlotte Zolotow Book

An Imprint of HarperCollins*Publishers*

The excerpt from "Not Waving But Drowning" on page 66, and the poem "In My Dreams" on page 96 are both taken from *Collected Poems of Stevie Smith*. Copyright © 1972 by Stevie Smith. Reprinted by permission of New Directions Publishing Corporation.

1   2   3   4   5   6   7   8   9   10
First Edition

Library of Congress Cataloging-in-Publication Data
Wersba, Barbara.
    You'll never guess the end : a novel / by Barbara Wersba.
        p.   cm.
    "A Charlotte Zolotow book."
    Summary: In the middle of a small and largely unnoticed nervous break-down, fifteen-year-old Joel tries to cope with the complications caused by his brother's sudden fame as a novelist, a devoted dog, and the kidnapping of his brother's former girlfriend.
    ISBN 0-06-020448-6. — ISBN 0-06-020449-4 (lib. bdg.)
    [1. Brothers—Fiction.   2. Kidnapping—Fiction.   3. New York (N.Y.)—Fiction.   4. Humorous stories.]   I. Title.
PZ7.W473Yo   1992   91-24771
[Fic]—dc20   CIP
                                                                                      AC

for Charlotte Zolotow

YOU'LL NEVER GUESS THE END

1

THE WHOLE THING started because my brother JJ wrote a book that got on *The New York Times* bestseller list. The book was called *Stirring Constantly* and it is the worst story I ever read in my life. It's a first person narrative done in the voice of a dumb blonde—a New Yorker named Merry Graves—and the big thing about Merry is that she does coke. She does it in the morning, and at night, in her apartment and at her job—and she loves it so much that she would do anything to get high. I mean, *anything*. The name Merry Graves, of course, is supposed to be symbolic—but the point I want to make here is that when JJ's book reached number two on the best-seller list, I knew for certain that life is not fair. My father had always assured me that life is not fair, but deep down I hadn't believed him. Then JJ's book hit the charts, and on top of that, *Manhattan* magazine called him the J. D. Salinger of the 1990's.

Manhattan did a whole article on JJ, with photographs, and the point of the article was that JJ was a prodigy. In other words, it was supposed to be astounding that anyone twenty years old could have produced a novel like *Stirring Constantly*. A miracle.

All this happened a year ago, when I was fifteen and not in the best of shape. I mean, I was right in the middle of having a small, silent, nervous breakdown—but if I had said that to my parents, they would have been shocked. Because I didn't look like I was having a breakdown. I looked fine. My name, by the way, is Joel, JJ's real name is Jonathan, and my father is Lou. My mother's name is Buffy and our dog is called Sherlock. And that's the whole family.

I had admired JJ until I was fourteen years old—

worshipped him, almost—and then I found out that he had been caught dealing coke. A very tiny amount, but nonetheless illegal. The whole thing was handled by Father, who's a lawyer, and JJ did Community Service instead of going to jail, but after that my feelings about him changed. I know how conventional I am, because JJ is always telling me so, but I just couldn't cope with the fact that my brother had been dealing drugs. He stopped dealing, but he also dropped out of Columbia University—where the incident had happened—and for six months, when he wasn't doing Community Service, he just slept. I'm not kidding you. All he did was watch television or sleep. And it was driving Father crazy. He had this illusion that JJ would go back to college and get a degree in Business Administration. But after the scandal, JJ dropped out.

Then—*then*—JJ's friend Bruno bet JJ a thousand bucks that he couldn't write a novel, a complete novel with a beginning, middle and end. And because JJ was broke, he took Bruno up on the deal and began to write *Stirring Constantly*. All of a sudden he was getting up at six in the morning and heading for the computer. All of a sudden he had a purpose in life. But the strangest part of it was that he would read me the manuscript, chapter by chapter, as though it was the Bible. "You'll never guess the end," he would say to me in hushed tones. "The ending is going to be a shocker."

But as far as I was concerned, the end was just as dumb as the beginning. Actually, there *is* no end. Merry just keeps on doing coke, and staying out all night at clubs, and sleeping around, and eventually she collapses and is sent to a rehab out West where she manages to . . . you guessed it. Where she manages to buy coke. Right in the middle of the rehab. From a nurse.

Before I go any farther with this, let me quote a section from the book. Just one little section and then maybe you'll know why JJ's newfound fame was upsetting me. Here's a part from Chapter One.

So I'm, like, trying to take a nap on the Fifth Avenue bus, on my way to work, right?, when this dude sits down next to me and begins to give me the eye. Fine, OK, I can deal with that, and anyway I'm trying to sleep for God's sake, but the dude just won't take his eyes off me. I mean, like, I have been out till four in the morning and now it is *eight* in the morning, and I am not a cheerful unit. And here is Mr. Right, trying to get friendly. Nice day, he says, as an opener. And I'm like, give me a break, I'm trying to get some shuteye here.

Then he goes, Do you have a match? And I go, What do you mean, a match? you can't smoke on the bus. I don't want to smoke on the bus, he goes, I want to set *fire* to it. And then he gives a little laugh.

I'm like, I don't believe this is happening. I mean, really! But then it occurs to me that maybe it *isn't* happening, maybe it's just a product of cocaine deficiency. I most definitely have this deficiency, and last night didn't help. I wanted to get wired out of my mind and all I got was bored. Because the blow that Ziggy sold us was about as effective as powdered sugar. So I open my purse and hand the dude a book of matches that says, "Hotel Pierre."

Because, like, if he's going to burn up the bus he should at least do it with matches that are chic.

The whole book is like that. Just one long, boring monologue delivered by a temporary typist named Merry Graves. And for this, JJ got on the best-seller list, became a celebrity, and got back in my parents' good graces.

Good graces doesn't even describe it. The minute that book was accepted by a publisher, my parents had a personality change. Whereas they had previously considered JJ the black sheep of the family, they now saw him as a star. A person who was suddenly being interviewed on television. A person whose book was in every bookstore window along Fifth Avenue. And then the paperback rights were sold to Dell, and then JJ's agent got him a film option from Paramount. And so, of course, it blew my parents' minds. "We should have *known* he was a writer," my mother would say to her friends over the phone. "He always wrote so well in prep school, and his marks in English were . . ."

By now you are probably thinking that I was

insanely jealous of JJ, but that wasn't it. A person doesn't have a nervous breakdown because of jealousy. No. I was falling apart because of the incredible unfairness of it all. I mean, I don't think my parents even *read* JJ's book—except for parts of it—because the content of the book didn't matter to them. All that mattered was that he had become a celebrity, overnight.

Television interviews, magazine interviews, calls from JJ's agent asking him if he would consider writing the screenplay for *Stirring Constantly*, because the guys at Paramount really wanted him to do it. Autographing parties at the Dalton bookstore. Lunches with his editor at The Lion's Head. And the phone ringing all day long. Because, incredibly enough, JJ was still living at home. It was easier for him to live at home, he told me. All the basics were taken care of.

Our apartment is on Fifth Avenue, in Manhattan, almost directly across the street from the Metropolitan Museum. It has four bedrooms and three baths, and a den and everything, so of course there was room for JJ there. But I thought it was a little odd that he continued to live at home. I mean, he was making a small fortune on that book.

And what was *I* doing during all of this? What was Joel doing while his brother hit the talk shows and gave wall-to-wall magazine interviews? Well, I was going to school—the Lincoln School on Ninety-sixth Street—and getting good grades, and walking the dog, and doing errands for my mother, and trying to help the homeless people in Central Park. With sandwiches and coffee. All of which, you have to admit, made me a very reliable person.

But that was the problem. I didn't want to be reliable. I wanted to be interesting, or dangerous, or heroic. Someone special, who stood out from the crowd. But JJ had beat me to it. The funny thing was that the minute he turned into a celebrity, JJ became organized. My brother, who in the past couldn't even get his socks to match, who was always late for appointments, whose main interest was going to clubs and meeting girls—my brother who never cracked a book in his life, but who was so smart he got straight *A*'s anyway—all of a sudden my wayward brother had turned into a one-man corporation. He got up at six and went to the computer, because of course he was now writing his second book—and he lunched with his editor and showed up on time for TV interviews. He began to dress well, in a beat-up sort of way—designer jeans and rumpled sports jackets, loafers without socks—and he had every hour of the day planned. So much time for writing, so much time for publicity, and very little time for girls. Which was the most amazing part of the whole thing. Because in the past JJ was second only to Casanova in trying to make out.

I must admit to you that JJ is handsome—black curly hair, piercing blue eyes, a broad grin—and I also have to admit that he is charming. Girls fall apart when they meet him, but until he started going with Marilyn Schumacher, most of JJ's dates were the sexual equivalent of fast food. Then he met Marilyn, and it was literally love at first sight—though I have to explain that the way he met her was odd.

It was early June, and JJ was traveling downtown in a cab on the FDR Drive, which runs along the East River. He was just emerging from that period where he had slept for six months. So there he was, sitting in the cab when a whole line of black limousines passed him. A wedding party. And in the biggest limo of all sat the bride, in a white dress with a wreath of flowers in her hair. For a few minutes the two cars ran parallel—JJ's cab and the bride's limo—and in those few minutes JJ fell in love. He told me later that he had never in his life seen a more beautiful girl than Marilyn. The only trouble was, she was on her way to a wedding. Her own.

"Follow that limo!" JJ said to the cab driver.

"What do you mean, follow the limo?" the cab driver replied. "I thought you wanted to go to Fifty-fifth Street."

"Never mind Fifty-fifth Street," said JJ. "Just follow that wedding party."

So the cab driver complies, and pretty soon JJ's cab *and* the wedding party are pulling up in front of a big church on Fifth Avenue. JJ gets out of his cab, goes into the church with everyone else, and sits down in a pew.

The bride, of course, has disappeared, into an antechamber or something. But the church is beginning to fill up with people, around a hundred of them, and the organist is playing soft music. The altar is decorated with flowers, and everyone looks cheerful and happy. That is, they look happy to begin with. After about an hour, they don't. What's happened? people begin to ask each other. Where's Robert? What could have happened? Oh, poor Marilyn. That girl must be a wreck.

As luck would have it—JJ's luck, I mean—the groom never shows up. Two hours pass and he doesn't show. Then, all of a sudden, the bride and her father appear and begin to hurry up the aisle of the church, towards the limo that is still sitting outside. The bride, Marilyn, is weeping and her father is red in the face. "I'll kill the bastard," he says. "Just let me get my hands on him."

And that's when JJ goes into action. Hurrying up the aisle behind the bride and her father, he reaches Marilyn and takes her by the arm. She turns in surprise, and he says, "My name is Jonathan Greenberg, and my heart goes out to you. Please—may I help you through this difficult time?"

Would you believe it, he scores. I mean, Marilyn takes one look at him, and all of a sudden she is not sorry that the groom never showed. She is just as attracted to JJ as he is to her. They stand there for a moment looking at each other—this tall blonde twenty-year-old girl, and JJ, who is only eighteen and a half at the time, but who looks older. "Sir," JJ says to the bride's father, "please let me buy you both a drink. The Plaza is nearby."

So the bride and her father—and JJ—get into the limo and go off to the Plaza Hotel, where JJ leads them to a quiet little table in the Palm Court. They assume that they know him, that he is somebody's friend or relative—I mean, he *was* in the church— so JJ doesn't disillusion them. "Let me order you a brandy, sir," JJ says to the bride's father. "And for you," he says to Marilyn, caressing her with his eyes, "a glass of sherry."

It turns out that their name is Schumacher, and it isn't long before JJ realizes that this is Donald Schumacher, the big New York tycoon. Donald Schumacher who has been busy buying up half of New York's real estate, and who has just purchased a major airline. Donald Schumacher who owns most of Atlantic City and is currently negotiating to buy Bloomingdale's department store. So not only has JJ fallen in love with a beautiful girl, he has also fallen in love with a rich one. Her mother is dead and her father is very indulgent towards her. Very devoted.

Within one week, JJ is sleeping with Marilyn and they are crazy about each other. Which, frankly, always amazed me because Marilyn is not too bright and—though she went to all the best schools—does not have the verbal style of Queen Elizabeth. Outside of men, her main interest is shopping. All she does with her friends is shop, take the stuff home, try it on, and return it for something else. But, I have to admit this, she is beautiful.

Then—after about eight months—JJ and Marilyn break up. Everyone is devastated about this, because they are considered to be the perfect couple. Also, during these eight months my parents and Mr. Schumacher have become friendly. They hope that JJ and Marilyn will get married. So everyone is devastated at the rift, though neither JJ nor Marilyn will reveal what happened. "We had a fight," is all JJ will tell anyone. "A disagreement."

Back to my parents. As I said, they were now treating JJ like he was made of glass, and he was busy writing his second book, *Call It Black*, which is about the spiritual crisis of a young bartender on the Upper East Side. The bartender leaves his job, goes down to SoHo to find out who he really is, and begins to paint. Thus, the title. It was June, I had just finished my sophomore year at Lincoln, and I was having a very quiet nervous breakdown which nobody seemed to notice. How could they notice? JJ occupied all of their waking hours. My father would even rush home from the office to see JJ on *Live at Five*. And there my parents would sit, glued to the TV, listening to JJ's opinions as though they were being delivered from a mountaintop. "I'm sorry," JJ would say to the interviewer, "but there really is no such thing as Yuppie Lit. I think it's sort of a disservice to my generation of writers to describe us that way."

I would sit there with them, listening to my brother expound—my brother who was a college dropout and minor criminal—and I would want to cry. Because it was *me*, Joel, who was showing up for life. Not JJ. Me, who didn't do drugs and who got good grades, who was kind to animals and fed the homeless people in the Park. Me, who had to work like crazy for everything he had, whether it was an *A* in English or a date with a girl. And nobody on the face of the earth gave a damn.

And then Marilyn Schumacher was kidnapped.

2

POOR MARILYN! She wasn't my favorite person in the world—and it had been months since JJ had seen her—but still, I didn't want to think of her as being kidnapped. Actually, Marilyn Schumacher had once been very kind to me. She had given me a hundred dollars towards the food I hand out in the Park, and she had even helped me distribute it one Saturday. Then we had taken a long walk with Sherlock, during which we had had a discussion about dogs. I prefer big dogs, whereas Marilyn seemed to like tiny ones, like Yorkies.

Since Marilyn was my brother's girlfriend, I felt a

little odd walking with her that day—as though we were doing something illicit—and when she suggested that we go to a sidewalk cafe, I felt even odder. But before I could protest, she had taken me and Sherlock to this trendy place on Columbus Avenue—and because it was summer, we both ordered iced cappuccino. As we drank it, I realized all over again how beautiful Marilyn was. Long blonde hair and eyes the color of blue marbles.

Marilyn sipped her cappuccino for a while, and then she took my hand and said, "I'm so depressed, Joel. God. I could commit suicide or something."

This alarmed me. "Why?" I asked. "What's happened?"

Marilyn sighed. "It's this way. I bought this pants suit at Bergdorf's, on sale, and when I got it home I realized that it was gross. Just too gross for words. So I tried to sell it to my friend Tracy, but she thought it was gross too. God. And it was on sale and everything. So now I'm stuck with it."

I just sat there—wondering why things like that meant so much to Marilyn, but also feeling sorry for her. Because one day, when she was forty or something, her good looks would all be gone and what would she have left? Her wardrobe. Her bridge games. Thirty shades of nail polish.

She was still holding my hand, which made me rather nervous. So I said, "Well, I'm sorry, Marilyn. I'm very sorry about the whole thing."

"It was purple," she said sadly. "The grossest color you ever saw."

Anyway—I was the first person in our family to hear about the kidnapping, because it came over a girl's radio in Central Park. I was sitting there on a bench with Sherlock, having just given him a long walk around the reservoir. I got Sherlock at the ASPCA a few years ago, and he is the best thing that ever happened to me—a large, jowly dog who is loving and patient and kind. I adopted him because he was the homeliest dog in the shelter—part bloodhound—and I felt sorry for him. Sherlock and I went to obedience class together, but he didn't do very well. Either he would sit with his back to the class, or fall asleep. The instructor told me that we should repeat the course—but Sherlock and I never went back because all I really wanted from him was friendship. Someone to ease my loneliness. Sherlock is an almost perfect dog, but he has one major fault—he drools.

At any rate, I was sitting on that park bench, daydreaming, when a news bulletin came over this fat girl's radio. She was sitting next to me listening to an old Beatles song, when suddenly the announcer said,

We interrupt this program to bring you the following bulletin. Fleet News has just learned that Marilyn Schumacher, the daughter of the well-known financier, was kidnapped this afternoon, in New York City, in front of Saks Fifth Avenue. Witnesses say that the young woman was dragged into a white delivery van and abducted. There has been no demand yet for ransom, but Fleet will keep you posted on further developments.

I sat there for a moment, stunned, as the radio returned to its music. Sherlock was asleep at my feet and the world was going on just as before. But I was shocked. All I could think of was what JJ would feel when he found out. And also my parents.

"Sherlock," I said, "something terrible has happened. We have to go home."

The minute we entered the apartment, I knew that my father was home, because the TV in the den was going. That's the only place he likes to watch television, and usually it is JJ he is watching. This afternoon was no different. Both of my parents were perched in front of the set watching JJ being interviewed on some news program. Just for the record here, my mother is in her forties but looks younger. She's small and chic. As for my dad, he's ten years older and very distinguished-looking. He's a self-made man, however, from Detroit.

JJ's friend Jenny Tamowitz was being interviewed with him on the "celebrities" segment of the show. She's a girl with crazy red hair who published a book called *Hot Pavements*. Like JJ's book, it was a best-seller.

JJ had been running one hand through his hair and it was rumpled. He seemed angry. "Now look," he was saying to the interviewer, "if you want to talk about the big boys, the really big boys—Fitzgerald and Hemingway, and that generation—you're talking about people who screwed up. I mean, they began to think that their myth was them. The life and the work became inter-changeable. And that's not what we're into at all. Not at all."

The interviewer turned to Jenny Tamowitz. "What do *you* think, Jenny? Do you agree with your colleague here?"

Jenny had a wad of gum in her mouth and was chewing on it thoughtfully. "Yeah," she said finally, "like, uh, I do. Like, he's got something there."

"I mean, I strongly suspect that people are just *waiting* for me to screw up," JJ declared. "Because when you're successful, you get an awful lot of flak. From the media, from other writers. Every-one."

"Yeah," said Jenny, still chewing away. "Flak. You get a lot."

My parents were so absorbed in all this that they didn't see me standing in the doorway. I cleared my throat. "Mom?" I said. "Dad?"

My mother turned around. "*Shh*, Joel. Your brother's on television."

"I know," I said, "but . . ."

"Quiet!" said my father. "We're listening to this."

So I just stood there as JJ went on and on about

success, and how enervating it was, and how everyone was waiting for him to screw up. I could hardly contain myself, because I wanted to tell my parents about Marilyn. But then I didn't have to—because right after JJ's interview, the anchorman came on with the news of Marilyn Schumacher's kidnapping. "Oh, my God," said my father. "I'll have to phone Don Schumacher. This is terrible."

"Was that program live?" I said to my mother. "Was JJ down at the studio?"

"Yes," said my mother, "so by now, he knows about it too. Oh, poor Marilyn! They'll probably want a fortune for her return."

My father, who had hurried out to the hallway, came back into the den. "I reached Don Schumacher on his car phone. He's in transit. The kidnappers have asked for a hundred thousand in ransom, but he's not going to pay it."

"Not pay it!" said my mother. "But why?"

My father sank down on a leather couch. "Because he thinks it's only the beginning of a long line of demands. What he thinks they really want is information on that defense project he's involved with in Washington. And that project is top secret.

He couldn't tell them if he wanted to."

"Then what will he do?" asked my mother.

"I don't know. But he's on his way to the District Attorney's office right now."

I was still standing there with Sherlock, who looked hungry. It was dinnertime. He wanted his Purina Dog Chow. "God," I said, "I wonder what JJ will say about this?"

"He'll be devastated," said my mother. "You wait and see."

She was wrong. Because around thirty minutes later, JJ burst into the apartment looking furious. He had taken a cab home from the TV studio. "That idiot!" he kept saying to me. "How could she do such a thing? How could she get herself kidnapped?"

"Well, it wasn't her *fault*," I replied. "It just happened."

"It is just like that little fool to get herself kidnapped. It's just the kind of thing she would do."

"She was simply shopping," I said. "At Saks."

"So what else is new? All she ever did was shop. Fifth Avenue *existed* because of her."

"That's not true," I said. We were sitting together

at the kitchen table while Hannah, our house-keeper, cooked dinner. JJ was drinking a beer.

"They'll find her," said Hannah cheerfully. "You just wait and see."

"She's probably dead by now," said JJ. "Floating in the East River."

"JJ," said Hannah, "you mustn't talk that way. You must hold a good thought."

"She's probably been sold into white slavery."

He poured himself another beer as Hannah fussed around the stove—taking the lids off pots and peering inside.

"So," JJ said to me after a while, "how was I?"

"I beg your pardon?" I said. I was still thinking about Marilyn.

"*On TV.* Didn't you watch?"

"Oh. Well, yes, I did. You were fine."

"The interviewer was a cretin. I couldn't believe he was asking such stupid questions. But I thought we handled them pretty well."

"Right."

"Jenny's not the most verbal person in the world, but I thought she registered."

As what? I wanted to say, but didn't. And all

through that evening—as JJ kept drinking beer, and my parents kept discussing the kidnapping, and Hannah kept saying uplifting things—all during that evening I thought about Marilyn. It was possible that she was lying in a basement somewhere, bound and gagged. It was possible that they had flown her out of the country. God, I thought, she could be *anywhere*. Anywhere in the world.

The thing that bothered me—hurt me, almost— was that JJ didn't seem to give a damn. He acted like the kidnapping was some personal failure of Marilyn's, and that she deserved the consequences. As for my parents, all they could talk about was the practical side of it. Would Don Schumacher pay the ransom? Would the loss of his daughter force him to give away defense secrets? Would the Pentagon become involved?

I lay in bed that night and pictured Marilyn. Marilyn who had given me a hundred dollars to feed the homeless people in the Park. I remembered how nice she had always been to Sherlock, and how she had once bought him a dog bed at Hammacher Schlemmer. I thought of how dumb she was, and how sad it was to be a dumb blonde, and how terrified she must be at this very moment. There was no one in the world, her father included, who probably cared enough to go to the ends of the earth to find Marilyn Schumacher.

No one but me.

3

"SO WHY DO you feel obliged to find this woman?" Solo Jones was asking me. He is a friend of mine who lives in Central Park. An old man.

"It's not that I feel obliged," I said to him. "I *want* to find her."

Solo turned his head away and spit out some tobacco he had been chewing. "Sounds to me like you want to be a big shot. To get even with that brother of yours."

He was leaning against the wooden packing box that is his home, I was sitting on a park bench, and

Sherlock was dozing at my feet. "That's not it at all," I said. "I like Marilyn. And I'm terribly worried about her."

Solo peered at me with his watery blue eyes. "I was a detective once. Did you know that?"

"No."

"Yep, a detective with the Fort Lauderdale police force. Solved many a crime for them. Was cited for bravery."

Unfortunately, it is not always possible to believe Solo. At varying times, he has told me that he was a pilot in the Second World War, a vaudeville star, and a newspaper reporter. He has also told me that he was married to a debutante and lived on Park Avenue. Still, we are friends, and in many ways I admire him. Winter and summer, he lives in back of the Metropolitan Museum in a packing case that stands on its side. Inside the case are a sleeping bag, a lot of books, and a kerosene lamp. On cold winter nights the cops force him to go to a men's shelter. But Solo prefers the Park.

"Those programs you see on television," said Solo, "things like *Miami Vice*. They don't come near the truth, not by a long shot."

"Where did you ever see *Miami Vice?*" I asked him.

"At the goddam shelter. They got a set there, and believe me, I am *up* on all the programs." His eyes brightened. "Listen, Joel, I wrote a letter to the Mayor yesterday. Want to read it?"

To tell you the truth, I would have preferred to talk about Marilyn. But, since Solo considers himself to be a great letter writer, I didn't want to hurt his feelings. He has written letters to people like Mike Wallace, Cher, and Vice President Quayle. "Sure," I said. "Hand it over."

I studied Solo's letter, which was written on a brown paper bag, and which was filled with statements like "The constitution of these here United States guarantees that a man may *sleep* where he wants," and "I assure you, Mister Mayor, that we the homeless who want to reside in the Park, instead of the dangerous shelters, will lobby one day to accrue our lawful rights." It went on and on.

"There's more to it," Solo said. "But I ran out of paper bags."

I gazed at him, feeling sad. It was June and yet Solo was wearing two pairs of trousers, two sweaters, and an old coat of my father's. I had swiped it from Dad's closet, and he had never missed it.

"That's a good letter," I said, "powerful. But listen, Solo, what I need from you is some advice. About Marilyn."

"Ah yes, the rich girl. Well, what are *they* doing about it? The big shots, the capitalists."

"The police are on the case. And also the District Attorney."

"So what do you want me to do? Sounds to me like the big shots have got the case practically solved."

"That's the trouble. They haven't. I mean, Marilyn's been gone for two days now, and there's not a clue. Not one scrap of evidence."

"I need time to think about this," said Solo. "I can't come up with a solution all at once. Need time to think."

"Why don't you eat your sandwich?" I suggested. "It's roast beef today."

Solo eyed the sandwich I had brought him. "Where'd you get this? That good deli on Eighty-sixth Street?"

"Right. And I brought you some cheesecake, too."

"No coffee?"

"Don't worry. The coffee's right here."

"I gotta be frank with you, Joel. Some of the stuff you bring me is not first-rate. But that deli on Eighty-sixth . . . that's OK. Did I ever tell you that I used to be a chef?"

"No," I said. "Not lately."

Solo took a bite of the sandwich. "Yep, I worked at a *cord blue* restaurant in Paris, France. Which is why I am just slightly particular about food."

Ten minutes later I was walking home with Sherlock, still feeling sad. Solo put up a good front, but he suffered—living outdoors.

Sherlock, who exists through his nose, was sniffing his way home, bush by bush, tree by tree. And once again he was pulling on the leash. Ever since we left obedience class he has been awful about leash work. But the trouble is, he needs a huge amount of exercise. More than I can give him.

I stood on the corner of Seventy-ninth Street, waiting for the light to change, and concentrated on Marilyn. Maybe if I used visualization, I could find her. I tried to picture that white van snatching her off the sidewalk, and then, very briefly, I saw it heading downtown towards Greenwich Village. Nope—it was heading for the Queens Midtown Tunnel now. Then it was gone.

JJ, whose heartlessness over the whole matter continued to amaze me, was certain Marilyn was dead. He had recently seen a TV program on kidnapping, and had announced to all of us that eighty percent of kidnap victims wind up dead, dismembered, and buried.

Actually, JJ's behavior shocked me more than Marilyn's disappearance. Because he had once been a sensitive person. Not organized, not disciplined, but a good human being. When I was little he would take me to the zoo, and to foreign films, and he would even pick me up after school so Hannah wouldn't have to do it. We'd walk home together holding hands—and not self-conscious about it—and sometimes we'd stop at Baskin-Robbins for an ice-cream cone. He was almost the epitome of the good older brother. But then he wrote that rotten novel and became famous—

and that was the end of the JJ I had known and loved.

"Sherlock," I said, "if I didn't have you, I'd kill myself." But Sherlock didn't hear me, being too involved with a fire hydrant.

When I got home that day, Mother and Father were having an impassioned discussion in their bedroom, with the door closed. And, since I am a born eavesdropper, I went up to the door to listen. I know that eavesdropping is a crummy thing to do, but I can't help it. It's the only way I ever learn anything.

"Look," my father was saying, "private detectives are out of the question. The police wouldn't tolerate it."

"Then why doesn't Don simply pay the ransom?" my mother asked.

"OK," said my father, "are you ready for this? I suspect he won't pay the ransom because the Mafia is involved. That story about defense secrets was simply a cover."

"*What*?"

"Don Schumacher couldn't have pulled off that

Atlantic City deal without the Mafia. So maybe it's them he's in trouble with."

"You've lost me," said my mother.

"For God's sake, Buffy, it's perfectly clear!"

"It isn't clear at all. I know that Atlantic City means gambling—but gambling is legal now."

"My God, you're naive," said my father. "Wherever there's gambling, you'll find the Mafia. And that includes Atlantic City."

"I don't know why you aren't willing to get involved," said my mother sadly. "You *loved* Marilyn. We all did."

"That isn't the point."

"JJ thinks she's dead by now."

"Well, that's a possibility. But if this thing *is* Mafia-related, then Don Schumacher is wise not to give in. Because the FBI might enter the case. And if they find out that Don is involved with the Mob, he'll never have a moment's peace. His financial empire will be investigated."

"You mean by a congressional committee?"

"Right. So you see, it's a mess."

I went to my room and sat down on the bed. This situation was much more complicated than I could have dreamed. The Mafia! God. I had seen movies about them, and those guys didn't fool around. Marilyn, I said silently, *where are you?*

That night at dinner, the subject of Marilyn didn't come up. My parents were concentrating on their food—a very good steak cooked by Hannah—and JJ was going on and on about the research he was doing down in SoHo for his second book, *Call It Black.*

"If I can pull this story off," he said to me, "it will probably be the beginning of a new genre. The 'downtown novel' or something like that."

"Right," I said.

"My agent thinks it's a gold mine. The whole downtown ambience."

"What's an ambience?" I asked.

JJ gave me a patient smile. "Ambience means atmosphere, Joel, and the downtown area is loaded with it. I mean, there's a brand-new culture beginning there. Even the sex is new."

My father looked up from his steak and potatoes. "How can sex be new?" he asked.

"What I'm trying to say," said JJ, "is that the downtown experience is wonderful material for a writer like me, because the whole subtext of the thing is real estate. Downtown, the person whose name is on the lease is king. People go to bed with each other because of *leases*, for God's sake, because of living space."

"Trish Cameron bought some very interesting jewelry downtown," said my mother. "In TriBeCa."

"Exactly," said JJ. "The arts are flourishing there. Fashion, photography, food . . ."

Later that evening I sat in front of the television in the den, watching a movie with my parents. But my mind was on Marilyn. I saw myself breaking down the door of a SoHo loft and rushing inside, only to find Marilyn on a couch, unconscious, drugged. I saw myself in an Atlantic City casino, bribing two gangsters for information. Then the scene changed and I was in Sicily, where Marilyn was being held by some Mafia thugs in a crude village hut. I saw myself pretending to be an American tourist. Map in hand, I walk up to the hut and knock on the door . . . but what the thugs don't know is that they are surrounded by the entire FBI, who I have somehow brought along.

I woke up from these daydreams and shook my

head. It was going to take more than fantasy to rescue Marilyn Schumacher. It was going to take
skill—the skill of a major detective—and I wasn't
sure that I had it.

4

I WAS SITTING at the kitchen table while Hannah beat up some batter for a cake she was making. We were talking about Marilyn.

"*My* suspicion is that she has been forced to change her identity," Hannah said. "They have probably dyed her hair and given her old clothes. She may be walking among us at this very moment."

"I don't get it," I said.

"I saw an old movie once, with Anne Sheridan, and that is exactly what happened to *her*. Some kidnappers changed her identity and dyed her hair.

Forced her to be someone else. Do you want to taste this batter, Joel?"

"No," I said. "Thanks anyway."

"When you were little, you always wanted to taste the batter."

"I know."

Just for the record here, Hannah is a very large person with white hair, which she pulls back into a bun. She wears orthopedic shoes, because her feet always hurt, and lately she has become involved with something called Scientific Religion. They hold meetings down on Forty-eighth Street.

"I've asked that our meeting tonight, down at the Center, be focused on Marilyn," Hannah said to me. "I've asked that we treat for her predicament."

"What does that mean, exactly? To treat for something?"

"Why Joel, I've explained that to you many times. We meditate on the person who is in trouble—in this case, Marilyn—and then we do a treatment for her. We use positive thinking to help her out."

"How could *thinking* help Marilyn Schumacher? She's been kidnapped."

"You better come to a meeting with me one night, Joel. Because, to tell you the truth, you are becoming a very negative person. When you were little, you were like a ray of sunshine. But now the world has gotten to you, and you're negative."

"I'm not."

"Oh, yes you are, and so is that brother of yours. All he keeps saying is that Marilyn is dead—whereas the truth is probably quite different. She may be walking among us at this very moment, disguised as a bag lady."

I tried to picture Marilyn as a bag lady, and failed. "Well," I said lamely, "I've got to go now. It's time for Sherlock's afternoon walk."

I made Sherlock "sit and stay" near the front door, while I looked for his leash. Then I got my knapsack, which was filled with sandwiches and donuts, and went down in the elevator.

"Heel!" I said to Sherlock, as we walked along Fifth Avenue. But the command fell on deaf ears. Sherlock had his nose pressed to the pavement and was following some kind of trail.

I handed out sandwiches to two old women named Maude and Mabel, who live on a park bench. I gave a sandwich and two donuts to a starved-looking kid who was sitting dejectedly on the grass. He looked like a runaway, so I handed him one of the cards I keep in my pocket. "The streets are tougher than you are," said the printed card. "For help, call Safety House, 555-6040."

While Solo Jones ate his sandwich, and Sherlock sat watching two kids playing ball, I thought about what Hannah had said. Was it possible that Marilyn had been forced to wear a disguise? Was it possible that she was walking among us with dyed hair?

Solo finished the food I had brought him, and leaned back against his packing case. "Did I ever tell you how I got the name Solo?" he asked.

"No," I said.

"Got it in the Second World War, when I was a fighter pilot. Would only go up alone, in one of those small Coker Two Hundreds—which is like a Spitfire, but even smaller. My buddies would go up in twos, and sometimes threes, but I was strictly a one-man operation. Lord almighty! Was decorated more times than I could count. The Bronze Medal, the Silver Star . . . Why Joel, I don't believe you are listening to me. What's the matter?"

"It's Marilyn," I said. "I'm still trying to find the solution."

"So you can be a big shot?"

"No!" I said angrily. "So I can save her life! It's been *four days* now, Solo, and they still don't know where she is. I've got to find a solution."

All of a sudden, Solo turned and looked at Sherlock. I mean, he looked at him like he had never seen him before. "Son," he said, "there's your solution. Right there. Sitting on the grass."

"What?"

"Didn't you once tell me that dog is a bloodhound?"

"Yes. But he's only part bloodhound. Three-quarters, maybe."

"Then you got three-quarters of your solution sitting right there. How come you never thought of that, Joel? Are you a moron?"

"I don't . . ."

"Listen to me!" said Solo Jones. "And don't you dare interrupt. What you have got there is a dog who is three-quarters bloodhound. And the purpose of bloodhounds is to find people! Didn't you know that? Every bloodhound is a mantrailer, and the reason I know this is that I was raised in a small town in Ohio, near a prison, and whenever one of those convicts would escape they'd set the hounds on him. Just like in the movies."

"But . . ."

"Hush now, and pay attention. No matter who it was the police wanted in those days, they'd use bloodhounds. Not that the breed is vicious, not at all. But Joel, they can follow a scent *hanging in midair*, it doesn't even have to be on the ground. Human beings leave their scent behind on the air."

"But . . ."

"I know, I know, your friend has been gone for some days now. But if you could get hold of one of her possessions, a piece of clothing maybe, and present it to that dog—why maybe he would lead you to her."

I stared at Solo. "That's fantastic."

"Not fantastic at all. Just the simple truth. You are the owner of a dog who is three-quarters bloodhound, and you didn't even think of it. Are you stupid, Joel? What's wrong with you?"

"Well," I said slowly, "it's a thought."

"It's more than a thought," said Solo, lighting a

cigarette butt. "It's your solution. Go buy yourself a book on bloodhounds and read up on the breed. Do some detective work. Just don't moon about like a debutante."

Two hours later I was locked in my room, along with Sherlock and a book whose title was *You and Your Bloodhound*. I would look at the photographs of bloodhounds, then look at Sherlock, and the resemblance was uncanny. He looked *exactly* like a bloodhound, and his characteristics—drooling, pulling on the leash, no road sense, a delicate stomach—were completely in line with the breed. I had bought the book at a small store in our neighborhood that specializes in books on gardening and dogs.

Solo may have been a liar about a lot of things, but as far as bloodhounds were concerned, he had hit the mark. It was absolutely true that they could follow a person's scent for miles and miles. They could even follow a scent when it had been interrupted—by someone getting into a car and traveling that way for a few hours—because their sense of smell was uncanny. A million times stronger than that of humans.

I studied Sherlock—appreciating his jowly face and sad eyes. His long ears and wrinkled brow. If I could get hold of some personal item of Marilyn's, would he be able to trace her? "You must trail from the scene of the crime," said the bloodhound book—which, in this case, meant Saks Fifth Avenue.

Solo thought I wanted to find Marilyn in order to be a big shot, but that wasn't it. The truth—the real truth—was simply that I was sick and tired of everyone belittling me. Either JJ was being patronizing, or Hannah was telling me I was negative, or Solo was commenting on how stupid I was. And my parents! All they ever said to me these days was, "Be quiet, your brother is on television." Or, "Look, Joel, here's an article on JJ in *Newsweek*!"

What I needed was some article that had belonged to Marilyn, something that had her scent on it. Then it hit me. I had keys to Marilyn Schumacher's apartment! Keys she had once loaned me so I could feed her cat while she was spending the weekend in the Hamptons with JJ. She had owned the cat for a few months, discovered she was allergic to it, and given it away to a friend. But I still had a set of keys to her apartment—the pied-à-terre she kept in the city because her father's house was way uptown, in Riverdale.

"Sherlock," I said, "we are about to go into the search-and-rescue business. I hope you're prepared." But Sherlock was busy chewing on a raw-hide bone, and paid no attention to me.

Late that afternoon, minus Sherlock, I walked over to Marilyn's apartment on East Eighty-fourth Street. It was a studio apartment in a brownstone, a walk-up, and I had keys to both the inner and outer doors. I was so nervous I was sweating—because it was possible that the cops were watching Marilyn's place night and day. They could have the whole neighborhood staked out, for all I knew.

I stood across the street from Marilyn's building and observed it for a while. There was a greenish light in the sky, as though it was about to rain, and people were starting to come home from work. Men with briefcases. Women carrying groceries. Little kids in their private-school uniforms. But I didn't see anyone watching the building. No one but me.

After a half hour, I took a deep breath and

crossed the street, unlocked the outer door of the building, and began to climb the stairs. Everything was quiet, and there were cooking smells in the air. Beef stew. Potatoes. Soon I was standing in front of Marilyn's door—3-B—key in hand.

I opened the door to the apartment and slipped inside. The shades were drawn, and the place looked eerie and strange. But then the scene became familiar—the white couch and white leather chairs, the big gilt mirror, the polished dining table. The apartment was one large room divided into sections. Marilyn's double bed, with its flowered spread, was neatly made.

Someone had been here before me, however—the cops, probably—because it wasn't long before I saw that bureau drawers and desk drawers were pulled open. The closet door was open too, and all of the cabinets in the tiny kitchen. Several photos in silver frames were lying on the couch—and one of these photos was of JJ.

Which article to choose for Sherlock? A sweater, a pair of gloves? No, I said to myself, a scarf. Marilyn wears a very strong perfume called *Cauchemar*, and that scent would be on a scarf.

I found one in a bureau drawer—a white silk scarf with a pattern of pink roses—and as I bent over to sniff it, I could smell *Cauchemar* very strongly. Following the instructions in my bloodhound book, I picked up the scarf with a pair of tweezers and put it into a Ziploc plastic bag. "Try to keep the scent article clear of your own scent," the book had said, in a chapter called "Mantrailing." "Use tweezers, a fork, even a stick to pick it up."

I closed the plastic bag and took one last look around the place. How empty it seemed without Marilyn! And how forlorn all her possessions looked, especially her collection of glass mice. Why would a person in her twenties need to collect glass mice? It was sort of childish. And touching. I walked to the door of the apartment, but still I didn't leave. There was something strange and compelling in the room, as though its occupant had just died.

I went down the three flights quickly, slipped out the front door, and hurried across the street—where I concealed myself in the entrance to a barbershop. It was dusk now, and streetlights were beginning to come on. A taxi pulled over to the curb, thinking I wanted a ride, but I shook my head. What I wanted to be sure of was that I wasn't being followed—that I was in the clear. And it seemed that I was until a man came hurrying down the block and headed straight for Marilyn's building. He was dressed like Humphrey Bogart in some old film—a belted raincoat, a hat with a broad brim—and before he entered the brownstone, he glanced around carefully, to the left and right. He was behaving just like a professional detective, or a maybe a caricature of one.

But it wasn't a detective at all. It was JJ.

5

THE NEXT MORNING, at eight A.M., I sat in the dining room having breakfast with my mother. Dad had left for the office early, and JJ was holed up in his room working at the computer. Hannah had just served us some pancakes, and I was pouring syrup on mine, when my mother said, "My Monday Discussion Group has decided to look for Marilyn."

"What?" I said. "What did you say?"

"I said, Joel, that my Monday Ladies' Group has decided to begin their own search. We've hired a psychic to come and help us. His name is Cleo Allen Hibbs."

"I don't get it."

"It's five days now, and from what Don Schumacher tells your father, there's not a clue about Marilyn. So my Ladies' Group is going to give it a try. It was Trish Cameron's idea."

Inwardly, I groaned. Because my mother's Discussion Group is a very annoying group of women. There are eight of them, and every Monday they meet at our apartment for lunch, and then they discuss a chosen topic. Nuclear war. Cocaine. Teenage pregnancy. Sometimes they have speakers, and other times they spend the whole afternoon writing letters to congressmen. They think of themselves as activists, which is crazy. But they do.

"How could a psychic find Marilyn?" I asked.

"Through clairvoyance, Joel. All Mr. Hibbs needs is a photo of Marilyn, and then he will go into a trance. He will try to picture where she is."

"Wow."

"It's done all the time," said my mother. "As a matter of fact, I'm surprised the police didn't use this method at the beginning."

I took a swallow of milk. "What does Dad think of it?"

"You know your father. He thinks we're just a

bunch of silly women. But wouldn't it be interesting if Mr. Hibbs could solve the case? Wouldn't it be wonderful?"

My mother kept on talking, but my mind had slipped back to the previous night, when, hiding in the barbershop doorway, I had seen JJ go into Marilyn's building. I had waited for him to come out for at least thirty minutes, and when he hadn't I had hurried home. But this new development was startling, because it meant that JJ was involved with the kidnapping. Either that, or he was gathering material for his next book, the one after *Call It Black*, which was going to be a mystery. "But not an ordinary mystery," he had declared. "More in the postmodern vein. You know, Joel. The kind where you know who the killer is from the very beginning, and then work your way backwards."

There were three possibilities. First, that JJ was involved in the kidnapping. Second, that he was simply gathering material for a book. Third, that he wanted to remove something from the apartment that might implicate him. God, I thought, I don't know JJ at all. All of us live here in the same household, but we do not know each other.

After breakfast, my mother went into her bedroom and came out with a book for me to read, a book by Cleo Allen Hibbs. It was called *The World of Clairvoyance*, and on the back flap was a photo of a little man who looked like a dwarf. Cleo Allen Hibbs, said the flap copy, was a famous psychic who had been born in Australia. He had appeared on the Donahue show.

I went into my room, placed the book on my bureau, and gazed at Sherlock. He was lying flat on his back, sound asleep, with his paws in the air. He did not look ready for search-and-rescue work. "Sherlock," I said, "wake up. We're starting work today."

A few minutes later, he and I were in a cab heading downtown. Cabs are my family's weakness. We take them everywhere, and JJ even took one to Connecticut once, to visit a girl named Gloria. He was seventeen at the time, and the cab cost two hundred dollars, but it didn't faze him because Gloria was a big deal—an actress who was starring in a play in Westport.

I had Marilyn's scarf with me, tightly enclosed in the Ziploc bag, and I also had my Swiss Army knife, a small pad and pencil, and a flashlight. The flashlight might not be necessary, but you never knew. Sherlock and I might be out after dark.

I was wearing jeans, a pale blue shirt, and a safari jacket I had bought at a place called Hunting World. It was beige cotton, and it had dozens of little pockets. I had never been able to figure out what the pockets were for—rolls of film, perhaps—but I felt it suited this occasion. I had also slicked back my curly hair and was wearing sunglasses—all of which made me feel more attractive than usual.

Sherlock was asleep on the seat beside me. "What kind of dog is that?" the cabbie asked, as we passed the Plaza Hotel. "A coonhound?"

"Uh, no," I said. "He's more bloodhound than anything else."

"My dog's a poodle," said the cabbie. "Purebred."

"No kidding?" I said politely.

"Yeah, a miniature poodle. The wife is crazy about him—named him Charles. The trouble is, we paper-trained him and now he will only go on paper. The wife takes him down to the street, she has to take a pile of newspapers with her. It's crazy."

The cabbie let us out at Fiftieth Street, across from Saks, and Sherlock and I stood there for a moment getting our bearings. It was one of those rare New York days when the sky is pure blue, and clouds are scudding by, and Rockefeller Center is filled with banks of flowers, and people look almost cheerful. An old lady came up to me and handed me a card that said, "Jesus Saves! Repent before it is too late." She seemed to want money for the card, so I gave her some change.

I crossed the street and stood in front of Saks Fifth Avenue. Sherlock still looked sleepy, and he didn't like the nylon harness he was wearing. It scratched. As usual, crowds of people were going in and out of Saks. We were in the way. People kept pushing past us.

I thought of Marilyn, who had probably been going to Saks that day to buy something very feminine. Some pantyhose, or a new shade of lipstick. And then—suddenly—I could see Marilyn very clearly. That long blonde hair. That beautiful figure. That funny little smile. She had gone to Miss Harrod's School for Girls on East Seventy-ninth Street, and was always saying that things were "too outrageous" or "too divine." All the girls from Miss Harrod's talk that way. It's a kind of dialect.

Using the tweezers I had brought along, I took Marilyn's silk scarf out of the plastic bag and thrust it in front of Sherlock's nose. "Sherlock," I said, "this belonged to Marilyn. Find her! Find Marilyn!"

Sherlock sniffed the scarf carefully, and then he looked up at me with his big brown eyes. He knew I wanted him to do *something*, but he wasn't sure what. Again, I waved the silk scarf in front of his nose. "Find Marilyn!" I said. "Find her!"

Just as I was beginning to think that Sherlock was retarded, he took off. Suddenly, he was pulling me around the corner towards Madison Avenue. Suddenly, he seemed alert. Straining at the harness, he dragged me across Madison and on to Park Avenue. Then we were heading towards St. Bartholomew's Church. I almost had to run to keep up with Sherlock, he seemed demented. Was it possible that after five days, he could smell Marilyn's perfume in the air? My bloodhound book had said that a person's scent is dispersed from his body like a mist, and then settles to the ground where it clings to things. Trees, shrubs, buildings.

Sherlock came to a halt in front of St. Bartholomew's and glanced at me. He looked confused. "A church?" I said to him. "You think she's inside a church?"

He sat down on the sidewalk. Then he lay down, and put his head on his paws. He seemed ready to go to sleep again. "Look Sherlock," I said, "this is a church. Are you sure you haven't made a mistake?"

Sherlock yawned and closed his eyes. He had forgotten all about Marilyn.

I stood looking at St. Bartholomew's. Was there any chance that Marilyn could be inside? Kidnapped by a minister? Held hostage in the rectory? Hypnotized, and forced to sing in the choir? No, it wasn't possible at all. Sherlock had made a mistake.

That night at dinner, I sat quietly with my family at the dinner table. I felt so discouraged that I had nothing to say to anyone. JJ, as usual, was going on and on about himself. About being invited to appear on the Larry King TV show. About being interviewed for *The New York Times*.

The phone rang in the hallway. My father went

to answer it, and when he came back there was an odd look on his face. "Listen to this," he said to the three of us. "There's been a break in the kidnapping case. That was Don on the phone."

"Oh, my Lord," said my mother. "What's happened?"

"He received a tip a few hours ago, a phone call from a woman with some kind of an accent. She said that Marilyn's being held in the theatre district. She also described what Marilyn was wearing on the day of the kidnapping, right down to the last detail. Shoes, stockings, a pink satin slip—everything."

I glanced sharply at JJ, to see how he would react to this news. His face was strangely impassive.

"Oh Lou," said my mother. "Does that mean she's dead?"

"Not at all," said my father. "What it probably means is that one of the kidnappers, this woman no doubt, is getting nervous. They don't know why Don isn't paying the ransom. They want to give him a shove."

"Why would they say where she is?" I asked. "I mean, why mention the theatre district?"

"There, you have me," said my father. "It's a ruse—but I'm not sure what kind."

Once again, I looked at JJ. His face was blank. But Hannah, who was standing in the doorway to the kitchen, seemed very agitated. "We did a treatment on this down at the Center," she said. "Just the other night. I *knew* it would work, I just knew it."

"Hannah, please . . ." said my mother.

"Because if you hold a good thought, that thought grows," Hannah declared. "It grows and s in a fruitful way."

is the first real lead Don's had," said my fa-o, Buffy, you'd better call off the psychic."

But Lou, I can't do that," said my mother. "We've hired him for Monday."

"You'll be wasting your money, sweetie. The case will be solved by then."

JJ rose abruptly to his feet. "I don't want any dessert," he said. "I think I'll go out to a movie."

I got up from the table, too. "Me neither. I have some reading to do."

I went to my room and closed the door. When I heard the front door slam—JJ going out—I waited for a few minutes, and then I followed him down in the elevator. When I reached the street he was standing in a phone booth on the corner, dialing a number. He spoke briefly into the phone, and then he hurried out of the booth and hailed a cab. Fortunately, a second cab appeared, which I flagged down. "Follow that cab in front of you," I said to the driver. "OK?"

I felt slightly ridiculous, like I was in the middle of a bad movie, but the driver didn't protest. "You got it," he said, and turned on the meter.

JJ's cab entered the Park at Seventy-ninth Street and began to make its way over to the West Side. Cautiously, my cab followed. Across Central Park West, past Columbus Avenue, up Riverside Drive. "I'm gonna hang back now," said my driver. "That cab is slowing down."

Which it did, right in front of an old apartment building on Riverside Drive and Ninety-fifth Street. There was someone waiting for JJ on the sidewalk there, a man in jeans and a sweater. He got into JJ's cab, and they took off.

"You still want me to tail them?" asked my driver. He was obviously enjoying the situation.

"Yes," I said.

"What is this, a drug case? You're a witness or something?"

"Right."

"Cocaine?"

"You've got it."

"Wow," said my driver. "I applaud your guts."

But then, everything went wrong. We were held up by a traffic accident between a cab and a bicycle. There was a detour because of road work being done on Broadway. And by the time my driver had extricated us from all this, JJ's cab was blocks away.

By the time we reached Broadway and Fifty-third Street, we had lost JJ entirely. My driver was more disappointed than I was. "Dammit!" he said. "We lost them. I don't know how it happened."

The meter said twenty dollars, so I asked the guy to pull over to the curb, lest I spend any more money. But one thing was certain—absolutely certain. JJ and his passenger had been heading for the theatre district.

6

FOR THE NEXT two days, Sherlock and I combed the theatre district of New York. Abandoning the idea that you must start from the scene of the crime, I simply covered all the streets in that area—giving Sherlock the scent of Marilyn's scarf every so often. Once, he led me into the lobby of the Shubert Theatre, where *A Chorus Line* was playing—and another time he led me into a place called Tony's Diner, on Eighth Avenue. It was clear that Sherlock didn't know what he was doing—but I couldn't bear to give up. I was convinced now, beyond the shadow of a doubt, that somewhere within this network of theatres and restaurants and hotels Marilyn Schumacher was being hidden.

Back and forth we went—from Sixth Avenue to Eighth Avenue, from The Winter Garden, where *Cats* was playing, all the way over to the Forty-sixth Street Theatre, where Dustin Hoffman was doing Shakespeare. And everywhere we went, there were homeless people. Sleeping in doorways. Pushing shopping carts full of junk. Begging for a few dollars. Some of them had dogs with them, on frayed ropes or leashes, and this was very depressing.

Every so often Sherlock would come to life and seem to be on the trail of something. I mean, he would prick up his ears and become interested in a particular locale. A shop, a restaurant, a newsstand. But none of it really amounted to anything, and then—as usual—Sherlock would go to sleep.

I had come to the conclusion that JJ had kid-napped Marilyn Schumacher. *Why* he had done this, I could not imagine, but all the evidence was leading to it. Had he done this out of revenge, be-cause of their breakup? Or was he simply greedy for the ransom—which Mr. Schumacher would probably have to pay soon. The minute I had seen JJ and his cohort heading towards the theatre district in that cab, I had felt he knew where Marilyn was. Could JJ be involved with the Mafia? Yes. JJ could be involved with anything.

Occasionally during those two days, as I walked from theatre to theatre, and restaurant to restaurant, I would tie Sherlock to a lamppost and go into a luncheonette for a cup of coffee. And sitting there at some counter, with cigarette smoke swirling around me and jumbled voices in the air, I would remember things about Marilyn. How she liked poetry and would sometimes quote a very interesting poet named Stevie Smith. How she had wanted to be an actress when she graduated Miss Harrod's, and had gone very briefly to acting school. When you came right down to it, I knew more about Marilyn than JJ did. JJ had been in love with her, but I had *observed her.* From the minute they started going together, I had watched Marilyn and taken mental notes.

Maybe it was because I never had a girlfriend of my own. But the only girl I ever dated seriously had turned out to be a disappointment, a girl named Kay Vandercreep. My school, Lincoln, is all boys—so we have these terrible dances with girls' schools three times a year, and at one of these dances I met Kay. She wasn't very attractive, and she didn't talk very much—but the idea that *anyone* should have to go through life with a name like Vandercreep saddened me. I mean, her name was not her fault. So I began to date Kay, only to discover that she was sort of lobotomized. She would agree with anything you said to her, no matter how crazy it was. I even said to her once—just as a test—that it wouldn't be long before the polar ice caps melted and all the port cities of America would be underwater. She nodded solemnly and said she agreed with me. And that is when I stopped dating her.

It was possible that I had been wrong about Marilyn. Maybe she wasn't as dumb as she seemed, or as shallow. And maybe—if she was eventually found murdered in some back alley—maybe then, we would reevaluate her. For how could anyone who liked the poetry of Stevie Smith be totally dumb? Stevie Smith's poems were the most unusual ones I knew, and my favorite one ended this way:

I was much too far out all my life
And not waving but drowning.

Poor Marilyn. She had not been waving at us, she had been drowning. Her silliness was a disguise for something else, some kind of tragedy. Her mother had died when she was five years old, and the only women in her life had been maids and governesses. It was possible that Marilyn thought the only value she had, the only *real* value, was sexual. Which would account for her obsession with her looks. Her obsession with department stores.

Then it was Monday, the eighth day of Marilyn's kidnapping, and my mother's Discussion Group was gathering at our apartment for the session with Cleo Allen Hibbs. I had skimmed through his book on clairvoyance—a book that had chapters with titles like, "You and Your Aura," and "The Body as Psychic Antenna"—and was pretty skeptical about the whole thing. So was my father. He had stayed home from the office on this particular day, however, to see Mr. Hibbs work.

I sat in my room with Sherlock while my parents and the ladies had lunch in the dining room. Every week someone contributes something to the meal—the salad, the dessert—and today they were all having homemade pecan pie. It wafted through the apartment, rousing Sherlock, briefly, out of his slumber. He was sleeping so much these days that I had decided to take him to the vet.

The ladies, and my father, all went into the living room, the doorbell rang, and then my mother was escorting Cleo Allen Hibbs into the apartment. He was the tiniest man I had ever seen—no more than five feet tall—and he was wearing a dark suit and a bow tie. His face was small and delicate. He looked like an elf.

I didn't want to be a part of this séance, or whatever it was going to be, so I stayed in the hallway—to watch from a distance.

My mother pulled the drapes in the living room, everyone sat on chairs in a circle, and then Mr. Hibbs gave a little speech. In a very quiet voice he explained that all of us are clairvoyant from birth, but that we never develop our abilities. "We all have antennas," said Mr. Hibbs, "psychic receptors, but we do not use them. We are spiritual TV sets, so to speak, gathering signals that are broadcast from beyond."

Mr. Hibbs asked my mother for Marilyn's photograph, and she gave him one that used to sit on JJ's bureau. It is a very nice picture, taken when she was around nineteen. A good likeness.

Mr. Hibbs studied the photo for a long time. Then he closed his eyes. He began to breathe deeply, and a little smile crossed his face. It was obvious that he was very relaxed. "I see . . ." he began.

Everyone leaned towards him, even my father. Even me, standing in the doorway.

"I see a harbor," said Mr. Hibbs. "A quaint and charming harbor on . . . Long Island. Yes, Long Island. There is a harbor, and sailboats at the dock . . . and a sign that says Long Wharf . . . and a fish restaurant nearby. I cannot . . . quite make out the name of the restaurant, but it is . . . still closed for the season. For . . . repairs. I do not see . . . Marilyn . . . yet . . . but the image of this restaurant is . . . compelling. Yes. A fish restaurant. On Long Island."

Mr. Hibbs came to a halt, and opened his eyes. My parents and the ladies from the Discussion Group looked dumbfounded. I didn't know if they looked that way because all Mr. Hibbs had come up with—for a fee of five hundred dollars—was a fish restaurant, or if they looked that way because they were impressed.

"Ah, is that all, Mr. Hibbs?" asked my mother.

Mr. Hibbs, looking more childish than ever, smiled. "Yes, dear lady. That is all."

"Well!" said my mother brightly. "That was just wonderful."

"Indeed it was!" said my mother's friend Trish. "Fascinating."

"Would you like some refreshment now, Mr. Hibbs?" said my mother. "A cup of tea? Some sherry?"

Mr. Hibbs, it turned out, did not drink tea. But he did drink scotch, and had at least three of them before he decided it was time to go. My father, exasperated by the whole event, had gone to the office—to rescue what was left of his day—but my mother was impressed. "I liked him," she said to me, when all of the ladies had gone. "I thought he was genuine."

"But what would Marilyn be doing in a fish restaurant on Long Island?" I asked her. "It doesn't make sense."

Smiling enigmatically, my mother began to collect ashtrays and coffee cups. "I don't know, Joel, but I'll tell you one thing. I'm going to find out."

She took a load of cups and ashtrays into the kitchen and then—on impulse—I picked up Marilyn's photo. It was fitted into an 8x10 ivory frame, and it was very lovely. In it, Marilyn was wearing a white fluffy sweater and a strand of pearls. Her eyes looked wonderful, and she had that funny little smile on her face, that smile I had never been able to decipher. I decided to take the photo to my room and keep it there for a while. No one would know the difference.

Later that night, around ten, I lay in bed with Sherlock trying to finish the bloodhound book. It was filled with court cases of missing persons who had been found by bloodhounds. "I wish you could read," I said to Sherlock. "You really need to read this book."

In the room next to mine—JJ's room—I could

hear my brother talking on the phone. He has a private line.

Eavesdropper that I am, I left Sherlock sleeping on the bed and stole out into the hallway. I pressed my ear against JJ's door. "I know," JJ was saying, "but there's nothing I can do about it. Look chum, you promised to make yourself available. It was your idea, not mine. . . . What do you want me to do, for God's sake, just give the whole thing up? . . . OK, OK. I'll call you tomorrow."

I hurried back to my room and closed the door. Then I sat down at my desk and studied Marilyn's photo. She looked so young and innocent in the photo that I could have cried. And the person who had betrayed her—betrayed all her trust—was my brother.

7

I WAS BEGINNING to see Marilyn Schumacher everywhere. On street corners and in the midst of crowds. In the Park, riding a bicycle. In the bookstore of the Metropolitan Museum. She was everywhere and nowhere, and that was the problem. It had now been eleven days.

I would get on the Madison Avenue bus, and just for a second, think it was Marilyn sitting in the back. I would go to Gristede's market, to buy groceries for Hannah, and imagine that Marilyn was wheeling a cart down near the vegetables. And on each of these occasions, my heart would turn over.

My heart would actually hurt.

I kept her picture in one of my bureau drawers, the bottom one, that was filled with T-shirts. And every evening, I would take it out of the drawer and look at it. "Where *are* you?" I would whisper. "Are you still alive?"

I kept thinking of that day, a year ago, when Marilyn and I had had cappuccino together. At a trendy little place on the West Side. She had talked about a pants suit she had bought on sale, a suit that turned out to be ugly. But the more I remembered our conversation, the more I felt that something had been going on beneath the surface. She had held my hand and looked deep into my eyes. She had told me she was depressed. . . . It was almost as though we were not talking about a pants suit at all, but about our inner lives. God! Why hadn't I responded?

I had been following JJ everywhere he went these days, but with no luck. He had simply been to three bookstores and the dentist. To his agent's office on Fifty-ninth Street. To his publisher. Once, he even caught me following him along Sixth Avenue, and had turned in surprise. "Joel?" he said. "I *thought* it was you. What are you doing here?"

"Uh," I said, "I have an appointment."

He looked at me curiously. "With whom?"

"A tutor! I'm being tutored in Spanish this summer. Don't you remember?"

The fact that JJ accepted this story, when I had never even *taken* Spanish, will show you how abstracted he was. But hell. If I had just arranged the kidnapping of my ex-girlfriend, I would be abstracted too.

As for Mother, she had done some detective work and learned that the only wharf on Long Island called Long Wharf is in Sag Harbor. So she and her Ladies' Group were arranging to go down there for a day, to look for Marilyn. My father thought this was absolutely crazy, but Mom wouldn't give in. She and Trish Cameron had hired a station wagon and a driver, and their whole group was going. "Look," said my father, "if by any chance you find Marilyn in a fish restaurant in Sag Harbor that is closed for repairs, I'll give you a thousand dollars. I mean it, Buffy. That's how crazy the whole thing is."

As for Hannah, she was still doing "treatments"

for Marilyn. And as for Solo Jones, he was still giving me advice about Sherlock. I was not giving Sherlock the right signals, he told me, which was why the dog couldn't accomplish anything. "You sure aren't much of a dog handler," Solo declared. "Though what you are good at, Joel, I don't know."

And then—out of the clear blue sky—I received a phone call.

It happened at five in the afternoon, and as luck would have it, no one was home but me. Mom had gone downtown to meet Dad at a cocktail party, JJ was at the dentist again, and it was Hannah's day off. Sherlock and I were sitting in the den, watching the five o'clock news on TV, when the phone rang. "Is this the Greenberg residence?" said a man's voice.

"Yes," I said, "it is. This is Joel speaking."

"Ah . . . is your brother home by any chance? JJ Greenberg?"

"No, he's not. I'm sorry."

There was a pause and then the voice said, "This is Robert Winkler speaking."

"Yes?"

"I am Robert. The person who was once engaged to Marilyn."

It took me a minute to catch my breath, and then I said, "How can I help you?"

"Well," said the man, who had a very prissy voice, "I don't know. I had hoped to speak to your brother."

I decided to take a leap into the unknown. "JJ is away at the moment, and so are my parents. Everyone is away. So maybe you could speak to me. I know quite a bit about the case."

The man sighed. "I've been calling Mr. Schumacher ever since the kidnapping, but I cannot get through. At the house, one gets a butler who is totally uncooperative. And at Mr. Schumacher's office, one gets a secretary. There is no way to communicate."

"Well," I said, "you can communicate with *me*. I know a lot about the case."

"There are things I would like to discuss, but I'm wary of phones these days. You never know whose phone is tapped."

"That's true," I said. "Why don't we meet somewhere? For a drink or something?"

"I don't drink," said Robert Winkler. "Nor do I

smoke. I'm sorry."

"Well actually, I don't drink either. We could meet anywhere."

"What about the Medieval Hall at the Metropolitan Museum?" said Robert. "There are benches there. We could talk."

"Right, right. When should I meet you?"

"Would this evening be convenient? The Museum is open tonight."

"I'll be there in a half hour," I said. "What do you look like?"

"Well . . ." said Robert, "I'm tall and thin, and I'll be carrying a book under my arm. *The Letters of Leonard Woolf.*"

I didn't know who Leonard Woolf was, but it didn't matter. "Right," I said.

"What do *you* look like?"

"Black curly hair, not too tall, blue jeans and a blue button-down shirt," I said. "See you soon."

I was very excited as I climbed the steps of the Museum thirty minutes later, though exactly why, I did not know. But there was something in Robert Winkler's voice that made me think he had information about the kidnapping. Whatever it was, it might be the lead I was looking for.

The Medieval Hall of the Metropolitan has always given me the creeps. There's a huge ornate gate there that used to be part of an old church, and bare polished floors, and little benches. The thing that has always made me uncomfortable is that it's so quiet. Deadly quiet. Like a tomb.

I entered the Hall and heard my footsteps echoing on the stone floors. For a moment, I couldn't see anyone. But then I noticed a man with a book under his arm sitting on one of the benches. "Robert?" I said in a whisper, and the man turned and rose to his feet.

He was older than I had expected, around thirty, but he was certainly tall and thin. Blond, but balding. Expensive clothes. We shook hands. "I'm Joel," I said.

Robert Winkler gazed at me. "I didn't realize you were so young."

"I'm not," I lied. "I'm eighteen."

I couldn't tell whether or not he believed me. "Shall we sit down?" he said.

We sat down together and I studied Robert a bit more. How could Marilyn have been engaged to him? He was so conservative. A banker or something. A Wall Street type.

"I'd like to get straight to the point, if you don't mind," said Robert, placing *The Letters of Leonard Woolf* between us on the bench.

"I don't mind at all," I said.

"It's this way. I've been trying to find Marilyn, but no one will cooperate with me. The police and the District Attorney turn a deaf ear. So I've hired a detective of my own—a man named Teddy Delucca."

"Why are you trying to find her?" I said. "If you don't mind my asking."

Robert looked at me in amazement. "*Why?* Because I was once engaged to Marilyn. I'm concerned about her."

"I don't want to be rude or anything," I said, "but my brother told me that, uh, you didn't show up for the wedding. I hope you don't mind my saying this."

A look of pain crossed Robert's face. "No, I don't mind at all. Because it's perfectly true. I did not show up. It's the only dishonorable thing I've ever done in my life, and the memory of it causes me grief. I *did*, however, send roses the next day and apologize to everyone. In the long run, it was all for the best. Marilyn and I were not compatible."

Then why did you become engaged? I wanted to say—but didn't. Instead, I said, "Are you a banker or something?"

Robert smiled. "No, I'm an editor at a publishing house. Harcourt Brace. I know your brother's work, of course, very well."

"Of course," I replied. And then, taking another leap, I said, "Do you mind if I ask you something?"

"Of course not."

"How did you know that JJ and Marilyn were going together?"

Robert hesitated. He picked up *The Letters of Leonard Woolf* and leafed through it for a moment. "Ashley Brooks told me. I assume that you know about Ashley?"

I shook my head.

"Ashley went with Marilyn before I did. He's an investment counselor, intelligent and all that, but a bit obsessive. He's still in love with her. He used to follow her all around New York."

I tried to take in this new piece of information.

"And you're in touch with him?"

"Yes. Actually, it was his idea to hire Teddy De-lucca. I mean, poor Ashley is suffering. . . . But the reason I asked you here tonight is that I need more information. I need to be told what's going on."

I paused, not sure that I should tell Robert Winkler anything. Because how did I know he was on the level? He looked like an honest person, but you never could tell.

Finally, I told him what I knew. About Mr. Schumacher being unwilling to pay the ransom. About the phone call concerning the theatre district. About a possible Mafia connection. I didn't mention Sherlock, however, because that seemed too personal.

When I had finished speaking, Robert looked baffled. "If what you are telling me is true, Joel, then Teddy Delucca's got it all wrong. *He* thinks that Marilyn is in Europe. A girl of her description was spotted on a Pan Am flight just the other day."

"No!" I said.

"It may not have been Marilyn, but the description matched. She was seen at Kennedy Airport boarding a flight to Paris with two older men.

Unsavory types, I might add."

"Mafia?"

"It's possible. I can't really say."

Suddenly, I felt exhausted. "I have to go home now," I said to Robert. "I have things to do."

We shook hands, and then he gave me his card. "Here's my business card, Joel. Will you stay in touch? Perhaps we can keep on sharing information until Marilyn is found."

"*If* she is found," I said tiredly.

Robert gave me a kind look. "Try not to be negative, old man. Negative thinking is like a virus—it spreads. Try to hold a good thought."

I should introduce this guy to Hannah, I said to myself. They'd really get along. Aloud, I said, "OK, Robert. Good luck."

"Good luck to *you,* Joel. And good night."

8

LATER THAT SAME night, I had a dream about Marilyn—and it was such a scary one that it woke me. I sat straight up in bed and clutched Sherlock. "No!" I said.

What I had been dreaming was that JJ, Robert Winkler, Ashley Brooks and the detective Teddy Delucca had all kidnapped Marilyn and were holding her hostage aboard an ocean liner. I had sneaked onto this liner and was going frantically from deck to deck, looking for her. Sherlock was with me, and he was sniffing his way through the boat—through dining rooms and recreation rooms, into a small movie theatre, and then into a network of kitchens and laundries. I had the feeling that time was running out, that Marilyn was about to be murdered, and that if we didn't find her . . .

It was then that I woke, my hand clutching Sherlock's collar.

"I need some warm milk," I said to him. "Do you want anything?" But Sherlock just yawned and went back to sleep. I have the feeling he rarely dreams.

I padded into the kitchen, heated some milk on the stove, and sat down at the kitchen table. Everyone was asleep, though there was some light showing underneath Hannah's door, which opens onto the kitchen. She was probably sitting up in bed reading *Scientific Religion, The Only Choice* by Edgar Grooms. It was her Bible.

Why had Marilyn had so many boyfriends? And why had each of the relationships failed? Was she promiscuous, or was it merely some desperate need for love? JJ had told me that she was wonderful in bed, which was something I could hardly bear to think about. Because I was all too aroused myself these days, by the thought of Marilyn. Her long blonde hair. Her perfume, pervading the silk scarf. That funny little smile . . . No wonder Ashley Brooks had been obsessed with her.

"Brooks," I said suddenly. "*Ashley Brooks!*"

Yes. It was possible that Ashley Brooks, who had been in love with Marilyn for years and followed her all over New York, was the kidnapper. He had helped Robert Winkler hire a detective merely as a blind. He was obsessed with Marilyn and had kidnapped her so that no other man could have her. He had paid two thugs to take her to Paris, on Pan Am, and was going to join her there. Was this as farfetched as it sounded? No. And it would exonerate JJ, whose actions these days were not really those of a kidnapper. He was spending a lot of time at the dentist, getting the gaps in his teeth fixed. He was taking cabs back and forth to SoHo, doing research for *Call It Black*. He was home every evening and went to bed early. The only thing that still worried me was that he had phone conversations that were terribly enigmatic. Conversations that were filled with sentences like "But I *told* you that was what it meant," and "If we don't cooperate, we won't be able to accomplish a thing."

I waited until seven that morning, and then I phoned Ashley Brooks. He was listed in the phone book, at a number way downtown. Centre Street.

I had a game plan as I dialed Ashley's number, only I wasn't sure it would work. I mean, people have told me I'm a pretty good actor, and once I played the part of an old man in a Chekhov play at school, and got rave reviews in the school paper. So I felt that my plan was worth a try. If it didn't work, I would simply hang up.

The phone rang and rang, and then a man picked it up. "Hello?" he mumbled.

"Brooks?" I said in a tough voice.

"Uh, yes. Hello?" said the man. He seemed to have a cold.

"Brooks, this is Marco Gambino. I'm calling about the girl."

"What? Who?"

"The *girl*, Brooks, don't give me none of your crap. The girl."

Ashley sneezed. "Are you calling about Marilyn? Who is this?"

"I just *told* you, fella, this is Gambino. I'm calling about the Schumacher girl."

There was another sneeze. "What?"

"If you've got her with you, you better tell us. And if you've sent her to Europe, you better tell us that too. Because we got a contract out on you, Brooks. You ain't long for this world."

"What are you *talking* about?" said Ashley. "Look—I have a terrible cold and my ears are stuffed up. I can't hear very well."

"It was us who was going to do the kidnapping, Brooks, not you. And then you come along and screw it up, right? But I'll tell you one thing. Either you tell us where she is, or we send the hit men."

There was a gasp on the other end of the phone. And then another sneeze. "But I don't know where she is! I swear it! I've got a detective looking for her right now."

"A likely story. Ha ha."

A suspicious note crept into Ashley's voice. "Who is this? Are you pulling my leg or something?"

"I repeat—ha ha."

"Look," said Ashley, "the minute you hang up, I am going to phone the police and have this call traced. I will not be intimidated this way!"

Suddenly, I realized I had made a mistake. A terrible mistake. Ashley Brooks wasn't the kidnapper at all. He was simply a businessman with a cold.

"Listen . . ." I said.

"Yes?"

"This is just a joke. I'm sorry. April Fool."

"But it isn't April! It's June!"

"I know," I said lamely. "I'm sorry. Look—go back to bed and take care of your cold, OK?"

And then I hung up the phone.

For the next two days, I slept. I don't know—maybe Sherlock's lethargy was catching, or maybe I was just depressed. But I pretended to be coming down with something and stayed in bed. Hannah brought me meals on a tray, and the doorman, George, walked Sherlock for me. Suddenly exhausted, I drifted in and out of sleep, having dreams in which Marilyn and Kay Vandercreep got all mixed up. Dreams in which Marilyn died. Dreams in which I married her . . . I saw myself in church that day—the day JJ met Marilyn—sitting in the congregation, waiting for the wedding to begin. But Robert never shows up, and people begin to whisper in alarm. Then I, Joel, step forward and offer to marry Marilyn. And then we are standing side by side at the altar as the minister smiles and says, "Dearly beloved, we are gathered here, in the sight of God . . ."

On Monday morning, around eight, JJ barged into my room. "Where's my picture of Marilyn?" he said. "Goddamit, Joel. Did you take it?"

I sat up in bed and rubbed my eyes. "Huh?"

"I am *asking* you if you took my picture of Marilyn. The one that Mother used for the séance, or whatever it was. That eight-by-ten photo."

JJ was still in his pajamas and looked wild. I couldn't figure it out. "Well, yes," I said. "I do have it. It's in my bureau."

"What the hell is it doing in there?"

Unable to think of an answer, I got out of bed and opened my bottom bureau drawer and took the photo out. "Here," I said, handing it to JJ. "I'm sorry."

And then something happened that was strange. Exceedingly strange. JJ took the photo from me and began to cry. All of a sudden there were tears running down his face. All of a sudden he was the old JJ—the person who used to have feelings. "Why the hell did you take her photo?" he said.

"It's all I have left."

He sat down on the side of my bed and wiped his eyes. "JJ . . ." I said, sitting down next to him. "Hey. I'm sorry."

"It's OK, kid. Forget it."

"No, really, JJ. I don't know how it got in there. I didn't mean to steal it."

"I know you didn't. It's OK."

But there were still tears running down his face, and the sight of them affected me so much that I took his hand. "They'll find her," I said. "They will. You'll see."

"It's been two weeks now. God knows where she is."

"I have faith, JJ. Really."

"You and Hannah."

"I didn't know you were so upset about it."

"*Upset?*" he said in a choked voice. "It's killing me. I can't work, I can't concentrate . . . and this new book I'm writing stinks, Joel. It really does."

"It does?" I said incredulously.

"It's false, and I don't know how to improve it. I don't know how to do anything."

I was still holding his hand. "Why do you

pretend not to care? About Marilyn, I mean."

He gave me a sad little smile. "I don't know. Maybe because she walked out on me. Pride, and all that."

"I thought *you* walked out on her."

"No, kiddo. It was the other way around."

"Could I ask you why?"

He turned a face to me that looked crumpled. It was the way he used to look when he was younger and some big disappointment had hit him. Not being elected president of his class. Not getting on the Yearbook Committee. "You really want to know?" he said.

"Yes, JJ. I do."

"She walked out on me because she met someone else at a party, a rock singer named Crash. He's very big with the young kids."

"I know," I said. "I've heard of him."

"And before me, there was the bridegroom Robert. And before Robert, there was someone named Ashley. You see, Joel, the girl just can't be faithful to anyone. Men are like Kleenex to her."

I decided to take a chance with JJ, a big one. "I've been eavesdropping on your phone conversations," I said. "They sound . . . mysterious."

JJ looked surprised. "Mysterious? Not at all. I've simply been talking to Bruno. He's trying to help me find Marilyn."

"*Bruno?*"

"My friend Bruno Kaufman. He's an actor, you know, and very familiar with the theatre district. Ever since that tip came in about Marilyn, he's been doing some legwork for me."

"God," I said.

"Bruno knows all kinds of people. Stage managers, ticket agents, bartenders. He knows the Broadway underworld, so to speak. But so far he hasn't come up with anything."

"Did you go to Marilyn's apartment once?" I asked him. "Dressed in a raincoat?"

"Why, yes, I was looking for clues. How did you know that?"

It was at this point that I decided not to tell JJ— ever—that I had thought he was the kidnapper. It would hurt him too much. "I was in the neighborhood that evening," I said. "I saw you."

There was silence for a while, and then I said, "I'm glad we had this talk. It means a lot to me."

JJ did something that absolutely floored me. "I love you," he said. After that, he left the room.

An hour later I was sitting in the kitchen having breakfast. Hannah had made me scrambled eggs and she was talking about Mother's ill-fated trip to Sag Harbor.

"You have to give her credit for trying," Hannah was saying. "Because it wasn't Mr. Hibbs' fault that there was no fish restaurant closed for repairs down in Sag Harbor. That was what he *saw* in his mind's eye. A fish restaurant closed for repairs."

"Right," I said, eating my eggs.

"What I always say is, nothing ventured, nothing gained. It's just a shame that that rented station wagon had to break down. But they got there! They held a good thought and got themselves all the way down to Sag Harbor."

My mind wandered back to Mother's horrible trip to Long Island—a trip during which the rented car broke down and all the ladies and their driver had to hitchhike on the expressway. Then there was a thunderstorm. And then Trish Cameron turned her ankle at this place called Long Wharf and they had to call for an ambulance. Late that afternoon Mom phoned Dad at the office, saying that she and all the ladies were at Southampton Hospital in the emergency room, waiting for a doctor to look at Trish's ankle, and they didn't know how to get home. He had told them to stay overnight in a motel, and had sent a limousine for them the next morning. But he was furious.

Hannah kept on talking, but my mind was far away—replaying the scene I had had with JJ. The last thing in the world I would ever have believed was that JJ was still in love with Marilyn. But he was.

"Joel," Hannah was saying, "you aren't listening."

I looked up from my scrambled eggs. "Huh?"

"I asked if you would do me a favor this morning. And you didn't even hear."

"I'm sorry."

"What I want to know is this. If I gave you cab fare, would you be willing to go down to the Metaphysical Bookstore and pick up a book for me? My feet are hurting so bad I just can't go anywhere."

"Where's the Metaphysical Bookstore?" I said.

"On Fourteenth Street, between Seventh and

Eighth avenues. Edgar Grooms' new book, *You Create Your Own Reality,* has just come in, and they are holding a copy for me."

"Well . . ."

"I'll give you cab fare each way, Joel, and when you come home there will be a plate of walnut brownies for you."

It was useless to say that I no longer had a passion for walnut brownies. Hannah still thought I was a little boy. "OK," I said. "Just give me a moment to get dressed."

Soon afterwards I was sitting in a cab with Sherlock, heading down Park Avenue. "The traffic is awful today," said the driver. "Park is our best bet. Park to Fourteenth Street, then straight across town."

"Right," I said.

I stared out the window, feeling more depressed than I had felt for days—thinking about Marilyn and all the people who had been in love with her. JJ, Robert Winkler, Ashley, and now the rock singer Crash. *How* she could be involved with such a person I could not imagine, because Crash was a psychopath. After every concert, he took out an axe and destroyed the stage.

I reached in my knapsack for a book I had just bought—the collected poems of Stevie Smith—and turned to a poem on page 129. It was called "In My Dreams."

> *In my dreams I am always saying goodbye*
> *and riding away,*
>   *Whither and why I know not nor do I care.*
>   *And the parting is sweet and the parting*
> *over is sweeter,*
>   *And sweetest of all is the night and the*
> *rushing air.*
>   *In my dreams they are always waving their*
> *hands and saying goodbye,*
>   *And they give me the stirrup cup and I smile*
> *as I drink,*
>   *I am glad the journey is set, I am glad I am*
> *going,*
>   *I am glad, I am glad, that my friends don't*
> *know what I think.*

That was the kind of poem my English teacher, Mr. Sharkey, would have called bittersweet. But everything about Marilyn was bittersweet to me now—since that scene with JJ. Poor JJ was suffering and I hadn't even known it. He thought his writing stank. And he had said that he loved me. . . . For one second my mind leapt forward five years. By then, JJ would be infatuated with someone else—but I, Joel, would still be there. Waiting for Marilyn and faithful to her. Forever faithful.

Sherlock was sitting on the taxi seat beside me, watching the world go by. He looked more lethargic, and more wrinkled, than ever—but when I had taken him to the vet, Dr. Hull had said there was nothing wrong with him. "He sleeps all the time because he is bored," Dr. Hull explained. "You must give him more to do."

The cab driver was playing classical music on his radio, which I found rather unusual, so I decided to ask him something—straight out of the blue. "Could I ask your opinion on something?" I said to him. "Would you mind?"

The man looked around and smiled. "Not at all. Shoot."

"Well . . . do you think six years' difference between two people makes a big difference? I mean, if the man is six years younger than the woman?"

The driver thought this over for a moment. "No," he said, "I don't. I mean, there's a line in a play by Shaw, where a young man says to an older woman he is in love with, 'In a hundred years, we will be the same age.'"

"God," I said, "that's terrific. What play is that from?"

"*Candida*. You ever read it?"

"No, actually I haven't."

"Go to the library and get it. It's good."

I was sorry when the cab pulled up in front of the Metaphysical Bookstore, because I would have liked to talk more to this person. "Are you a writer or something?" I asked him, as I paid the fare.

He shook his head. "No, I'm an actor. Between engagements, as they say."

"Well, good luck," I said to him. "Good luck."

The Metaphysical Bookstore was a very weird place—with incense burning, and wind chimes tinkling in the air, and rows and rows of books about religion and philosophy. Hannah had given me twenty dollars to pay for her book, which they were keeping for her behind the counter.

With *You Create Your Own Reality* under my

arm, and Sherlock leading me along Fourteenth Street, I decided to explore the neighborhood. I had never been down here before, and it was kind of interesting. Spanish restaurants and bars, markets, old brownstones. I continued west, looking in store windows and appreciating the fact that it was a clear, cool day. You could hear tugboats hooting on the river. A helicopter whizzed by right over my head.

And then Sherlock had a fit.

I'm not kidding you. Without any warning, Sherlock began to go crazy. With his nose to the ground, he pulled me straight across the street—right in the midst of traffic—and then he began to move in circles. "What's the *matter* with you?" I said to him. "Have you lost your mind? What's going on?"

He had dragged me over to a seedy-looking hotel called the Europa, and he was going round and round in circles on the pavement. His tail was wagging frantically and he seemed terribly aroused. And then I understood what was happening to Sherlock. Marilyn was inside this building. He had found her.

For one moment a passage from the bloodhound book came into my mind—a passage that
said that bloodhounds can hold scents for a long
time, store them in their memory—and then I al-
lowed Sherlock to yank me into the hotel. His tail
was wagging a mile a minute and he was trembling
with excitement.

Quickly, I took in my surroundings. A small,
crummy hotel lobby. No one behind the front
desk. A few worn leather couches and standing
ashtrays. Very low lighting, as if all the light bulbs
were forty watts or something. But not a soul to be
seen.

Sherlock was dragging me up the stairs—there
didn't seem to be an elevator—past the second
floor and on towards the third. And because I was
certain he had picked up Marilyn's scent, my heart
was pounding like a hammer. As a matter of fact, I
felt like I was going to pass out—that's how
shocked I was by what was happening.

We reached the third floor of the hotel and
Sherlock pulled me over to a door that said "355."
And then he did something I had never seen him
do before—he bayed. He did not bark, he did not

growl, he threw back his head and bayed. Like a hound baying at the moon.

It was a terrible sound, and he kept right on doing it. The door of 355 was thrown open and two men appeared. "What's going on here?" one of them said to me.

They were both short and fat, and both of them needed a shave. The one that had spoken was looking at Sherlock in amazement. "What the hell is going on?" he said.

I looked beyond him, into the hotel room, and there was Marilyn. She was sitting on a couch wearing a bathrobe—and her face was as pale as a ghost.

9

I LOOKED AT MARILYN and she looked at me. Then she let out a little cry, rushed towards me, and threw herself into my arms. "Joel!" she said. "Oh my God, it's Joel!"

"Who's Joel?" said the first man.

"Yeah," said the second man. "Who is this?"

"It's Joel Greenberg," said Marilyn, starting to cry. "My friend Joel."

"Get in here!" said the first man to me. "Fast! The dog too."

He pulled Sherlock and me into the hotel room. It was a shabby place, littered with newspapers and magazines and coffee cups. A color TV set was playing.

Marilyn was still crying. "Oh God, Joel," she said. "How did you find me?"

"It was Sherlock," I said. "He's a bloodhound."

The first man grabbed my shoulder and spun me around. "Who's with you? *Talk*."

"Nobody's with me," I said. "I came alone."

"You better be telling the truth!" said the second man.

"It *is* the truth. I'm alone. I didn't bring the cops or anything."

The first man was looking out of the window, down at the street. "I think it's OK," he said to the second man. "I think he's alone."

"Are you alone, Joel?" asked Marilyn. "Really?"

"Look," I said to the three of them, "I'm *alone*. Nobody came with me. Just Sherlock. He picked up your scent by accident, Marilyn. On Fourteenth Street."

The second man was staring at me menacingly. I wondered if he had a gun. If they *both* had guns.

Marilyn ran one hand through her hair. She didn't have any makeup on, and she looked exhausted. "Joel dear," she said, "this is Solly, and this is his brother Mike. They run a dry cleaning store on Eighty-sixth Street."

"Uh, how do you do?" I said to the two men. Grudgingly, Solly shook hands with me. Mike was still looking out the window.

"Would you like a Coke, Joel dear?" said Marilyn. "There's a little fridge in the other room. We have Coke and beer and orange juice."

I peered beyond her, into a bedroom. The place was larger than I thought—a living room, two bedrooms, and a bath.

Marilyn opened a box of Pepperidge Farm cookies. "A cookie, Joel?"

I stared at her. "Marilyn," I said, "what's going on here? Are you being kidnapped or what?"

She gave me her funny little smile, the smile I had been dreaming about for two weeks. "Well, yes and no, Joel. It's complicated."

"That's the word for it all right," said Solly. "Complicated." He went over and stood with his brother by the window. He seemed discouraged.

"Solly," said Marilyn, "would you mind if I

explained things to Joel? He's my ex-boyfriend's brother."

"Explain away," said Solly. "I don't care. Do *you* care, Mike?"

Mike had slumped into a chair by the window. "At this point," he said, "I don't care about nothing."

Marilyn took my hand and pulled me down with her on the couch. "Joel, what's happened here is just too gross. I mean, it's the grossest situation I've ever been in."

"Just answer one question for me," I said. "Are you being kidnapped or not?"

Marilyn frowned. "Well, yes and no. Sort of."

"I don't get it!"

"Now Joel, there is no reason to get mad. I'm trying to explain as best I can. You see, a couple of months ago I lost fifty thousand dollars. At bridge."

"What?"

"I was playing bridge at this woman's house, Bunny Hornblow, and we were all drinking white wine, and the stakes got sort of high. I mean, they got higher than usual. And I lost fifty thousand.

And I didn't know what to do."

"Yes?" I said.

"So I decided that the only way to get fifty thousand dollars would be to have myself kidnapped."

"WHAT?"

"Joel, please! Lower your voice. Don't make Mike and Solly mad. . . . Anyway, I decided to have myself kidnapped and get Daddy to pay the ransom. But it hasn't worked out very well. It's just the dumbest situation I've ever been in."

I looked at Marilyn, and in one instant all my fantasies about her disappeared. She was simply Marilyn again. Marilyn Schumacher. "Go on," I said.

"Solly and Mike are my dry cleaners, on Eighty-sixth Street. Do you know their store, Joel? Solly's Laundry and Dry Cleaners?"

"No."

"Well anyway, I have always taken my cleaning there. But several months ago they had a fire in the back of the shop, and they weren't covered by insurance. Their policy had lapsed and everything, and they were very upset. So I proposed this deal to them. About the kidnapping."

"Go on, Marilyn."

"What they needed to repair the fire damage was fifty thousand. And *I* needed fifty thousand to repay my gambling debt to Mrs. Hornblow. She's a very prominent woman, Joel. I mean, I couldn't *not* pay her. So what I decided was that we would ask for a hundred thousand in ransom and that Solly and Mike would kidnap me in their dry cleaning van and bring me here. Their brother-in-law owns this hotel. . . . So they took the sign off the van, and changed the license plates and everything, and kidnapped me. It was all arranged. They even brought my overnight case with my stuff in it."

I was looking at Marilyn as though for the first time. "Yes?"

"But it hasn't worked out very well, because Daddy hasn't paid the ransom. Solly phoned him and told him to leave the money in a locker at Grand Central Station, but he didn't do it. Imagine Daddy not being willing to ransom me! It's hard to believe."

"There was a tip," I said. "Some woman with an accent phoned your father and said you were being held in the theatre district."

Marilyn giggled. "That was me, calling from the

pay phone downstairs. I used a foreign accent. Solly and Mike were getting angry about no ransom showing up."

"But why did you say you were in the theatre district?"

"To throw the police off our trail."

Marilyn, I wanted to say, no one has been *on* your trail, so don't worry. Instead, I said, "Well Marilyn, since none of this has worked out, why don't you just go home?"

"I can't," she said sadly. "Solly and Mike won't let me. They're really angry now and want that ransom money."

I looked around the room, at the shabby furniture and ashtrays filled with cigarette butts. At the remains of a Chinese dinner. "You mean you haven't been out of here in two weeks?"

"Only to get my hair done," said Marilyn. "Solly took me to a beauty parlor downstairs, but it was awful. They used the grossest kind of setting lotion you can imagine. And then they did my nails the wrong color."

"Well," I said. "Where do we go from here?"

"I don't know, Joel, because now they'll hold you prisoner too."

"They can't do that! It's ridiculous!"

I marched over to Solly and Mike who were still gazing out the window. "Pigeons," Mike said, "the whole goddam city is filled with pigeons."

"I beg your pardon?" I said.

"What's ruining this city is pigeons. They leave their mess on everything and it corrodes the buildings. I read that in the newspaper."

"He's right," said Solly. "Between the pigeons and the drug dealers, this city is going to hell. If we was smart, we'd be in Florida."

"Florida?" I said.

"Who needs all this?" said Solly. "In the winters you freeze. In the summers you sweat. All you've got here is pigeons and drugs and lousy weather. Who needs it? Where we should all be is Pompano Beach."

"Look," I said, "I'm not entirely sure what's going on here, but I have to go home."

Solly gave me an odd look. "Home? You won't be going home for a long time, kid. So just sit down and relax. Take a load off."

I glanced at my watch. It was already midafternoon. "But my dog needs his dinner."

"So we'll go out and buy him some dog food."

"And then he'll need a walk."

"So we'll walk him."

"I'm sorry," I said, "but I really cannot stay any longer. I have things to do."

Mike rose to his feet and put his arm around my shoulder. "Look," he said, "can I ask you something? Something personal?"

"Well, yes," I replied. "What?"

"Can you tell me why this girl's father ain't paying the ransom? What kind of a father is that, won't ransom his own kid? Solly and me were *counting* on this money—not only to repair the shop, but to take a little vacation. Pompano Beach, Sarasota, something like that."

"Well . . ."

"We go to all this trouble to kidnap this girl, and then her old man won't pay!"

"Actually . . ."

"We even figure out how to do the ransom money. I mean, we rent a locker in Grand Central and then we send Schumacher a duplicate key. We know, of course, that the cops will be watching that locker night and day, so we get Solly a phony I.D. from a hood we know—a nice guy, actually, lives in Queens—a phony I.D. as a private detective. So after introducing himself to the cops, Solly has free access to this locker. He's practically one of the boys down there, checking on the locker every night. Pretty good, huh? Solly saw the whole thing in an old Jimmy Cagney film."

"Well . . ."

"Weeks of thought and planning, and then what happens? Old man Schumacher won't pay."

After that, things got very strange. Solly went out to buy some dog food for Sherlock, Marilyn sat in front of the TV taking polish off her nails, and after Sherlock had eaten, Solly took him down to the street for a walk. Then Mike brought in cheeseburgers and malteds, and then Marilyn read aloud to us from *TV Guide*, to see what programs we wanted to watch that night.

"You know what floor you're on, don't you?" Mike said to me, as he finished his cheeseburger. "The third. And this room ain't got a phone. So don't think of escaping from here, kiddo. We all stay put until the ransom comes through. Solly goes uptown to check the locker at Grand Central every night."

Which Solly did, at ten that evening. But all I could think about—as Marilyn sat in front of the TV, and Mike read the *Daily News*—was what my parents would feel when they discovered me missing. My parents, and Hannah, and JJ.

10

I HAD A LOT of trouble sleeping that night. The living room couch was comfortable enough, and Solly had given me a blanket and pillow, but I was filled with anxiety. There was a neon sign across the street that kept flashing into my room, and the sounds of traffic were very loud—much louder than they are at home. Marilyn was asleep in one of the bedrooms while Solly and Mike shared the other. Sherlock, who seemed quite at home here, was snoring on the floor.

I was dozing fitfully when someone sat down at the foot of the couch. "Shh," said Marilyn. "Shh,

Joel. It's me."

"You scared me!" I said.

"I'm sorry, Joel dear, but I simply have to talk to you. I can't sleep."

"Me neither. I'm very upset."

Marilyn took my hand and held it for a moment. She was wearing pajamas with little elephants on them. They were not attractive. "Joel? How are we going to get out of here? Do you have any ideas?"

I thought for a moment. "No."

"I mean, at *this* point, I wouldn't mind being found. I even threw a note out of the window yesterday, but nobody saw it. It just sat there on the sidewalk. And then it blew away."

I sat up on the couch. "There's something I don't understand."

"Yes, Joel? What?"

"Why did Solly and Mike let you go out to a beauty parlor? You could have screamed for help."

"The beauty parlor is owned by their sister, who is married to the owner of this hotel. They're all in on the deal. They all want to go to Florida."

"Is there a fire escape outside these rooms?"

"No. And three stories is much too far to jump.

The situation is just too outrageous. . . . I suppose JJ is laughing his head off these days. About the kidnapping."

I looked at Marilyn as the neon sign illuminated her face. "He's not laughing at all. Actually, Marilyn . . . he's still in love with you."

Marilyn seemed to go pale. "He is? How do you know?"

"We had a long talk and he told me that he still cares for you. He even cried."

Marilyn looked stunned. "He *cried*? JJ?"

"Yes, but you hurt his feelings, walking out on him that way. For that singer."

"But that was nothing, Joel! It didn't even last a month."

"Huh?"

"I met Crash at this party downtown in SoHo and he came on very strongly to me. And he was famous and everything, so I went out with him for a few weeks. But he's a *very* gross person, Joel, he never washes. And I'm not exactly a groupie."

"It's true," I said. "You're not."

"And I couldn't stand his music. I mean, I'm into music as much as the next person, but Crash is just too outrageous. At one of his concerts, he peed on his guitar."

"God."

"Right in front of six thousand people."

"Couldn't you and JJ have gotten back together? Afterwards?"

"No. He was furious about the whole thing. I mean, JJ is really very jealous. It's amazing how jealous he is. With everyone."

"I never noticed that."

"Well, he is."

"Listen Marilyn, do Mike and Solly ever go out together? Do they ever leave you here alone?"

"Why, yes. Every morning they go out to get breakfast and the newspapers. And sometimes they stop off at a barbershop for a shave. But they always lock me in."

"How long do they stay away?"

"I don't know . . . around an hour, maybe. Why?"

"Well, maybe today, while they're gone, I could lower you out of the window. On some bed sheets. And you could go to the police."

Marilyn thought this over for a while. "I don't

think I could do that, Joel. I'm scared of heights."

"Then you could lower me."

"I couldn't do that! I'm not strong enough."

As though we were two minds with but a single thought, both of us looked at Sherlock, who was snoring peacefully on the floor. "OK," I said. "We'll lower *him*."

"Sherlock?"

"Sure! Why not? I'll tie a note to his collar, saying where we are. I'll tell him to go home."

"Would he do that? Go home, I mean."

"He might."

"All the way to Eighty-second Street?"

"Why not?"

"I don't know . . . it's just so far. And Joel, please forgive me for saying this, but I never thought that dog was too bright."

For some reason, this made me furious. "Have you got a better suggestion?" I asked. "Because if you do, Marilyn, I'd like to hear it."

"Well . . ."

"Go back to bed. We'll talk again in the morning."

Marilyn padded back to her room, but by now I

was wide awake and knew that I couldn't sleep anymore. But my idea seemed entirely possible. We would make a rope of some bed sheets, wrap Sherlock in it, and lower him down to the sidewalk. I would tell him to "go home," and hope for the best. The only thing that worried me was that Sherlock doesn't have much road sense. He walks right into traffic, unless you rein him in.

Around eight that morning, Solly made coffee for the four of us on his Coffee Master, and then he announced that he and Mike were going to get us some breakfast. "There's a McDonald's right around the corner," he said to me. "What do you want? Scrambled eggs? Pancakes?"

"Pancakes would be fine," I said. "But I need to walk Sherlock now. He needs to go out."

"Oh, no you don't, kiddo. *I'll* walk him. I don't trust you as far as I can throw you."

Solly took Sherlock down to the street and returned quickly. "He did everything," he said. "He was a good boy."

"Do you like dogs?" I asked Solly.

"Sure, why not? They're OK. They don't hurt nobody."

Finally, Solly and Mike left—locking the door behind them. "Marilyn?" I said. "Let's go to work."

Marilyn went into the bedroom and stripped the beds. Then we twisted the sheets into ropes and made a sling at one end, for Sherlock. I put Sherlock inside the sling and tightened it around his stomach. He looked at me as though I was crazy.

I walked over to the window and looked down. How far it was! And suppose Sherlock slipped out of the sling and got killed? "This is not going to be easy," I said to Marilyn.

She was gazing down too. "It makes me dizzy just to *look*. Suppose he wiggles out of the sling or something?"

"Do you believe in God?" I asked her.

"I don't know. Sometimes."

"Well, if you believe this morning, then pray. Just say a prayer that he'll make it."

I tightened the sling around Sherlock's stomach. Then I took the note I had written and pinned it to the inside of his collar with one of Marilyn's hairpins. "Attention!" said the note. "Marilyn S. and I are being held at the Hotel Europa on West 14th Street. Room 355. Please bring police at once.

Joel Greenberg."

The look on Sherlock's face, as Marilyn and I dangled him out of the window, was terrible. It was a look of shock, mingled with fear, mingled with pure amazement that I could be doing such a thing to him. My heart almost broke as I saw this look, but I kept on lowering him toward the street. He was awfully heavy.

"Go home!" I said, as Marilyn and I lowered him inch by inch. "Sherlock, I want you to *go home*. Eighty-second Street, Sherlock. *Home.*"

For one moment, dangling in midair, Sherlock seemed about to slip out of the sling. But then, thank God, his feet were on the pavement and he was wriggling out of the bed sheets. With a curious look on his face, he stared up at us—three stories above. "Go home!" I said urgently. "Please, Sherlock. *Home!*"

And then he took off.

"I don't believe it!" I said to Marilyn. "He's even going in the right direction."

"It's true!" she said. "He's heading east."

"Pray, just *pray* that he makes it. It's a long journey."

We hung out of the window watching Sherlock until we could no longer see him. He was heading towards Fifth Avenue, going at a gallop.

"If he gets killed by traffic, I will never forgive myself," I said. "It will haunt me for the rest of my life."

Marilyn gathered up the sheets and took them into the bedrooms, where she made all the beds. Then she came back to the living room and sat down on the couch. She was still wearing her pajamas with elephants on them, and her mascara was smeared. She did not look too wonderful. "Joel?" she said after a minute.

"Yes?"

"When Solly and Mike come back, what do we tell them? About Sherlock, I mean."

I stared at her. "God. I don't know. I didn't think of that."

"I mean, how can we possibly explain his disappearance. What should we say?"

I sat down next to her, and took a mouthful of coffee out of someone's cup. "Well . . ." I began. But nothing came to mind.

"We'll just have to say that he fell out of the

window and was killed," Marilyn said firmly. "He died."

"Then where's his body?"

"Umm . . . well, maybe someone took it away. The police or the fire department or somebody."

"No good."

"Then what would you *suggest,* Joel? That we say he vanished into thin air?"

"I'm going to take a bath," I said to her. "I always think better in the bathtub."

I went into the bathroom and turned on the tub, and, finding a package of bubble bath there, I poured some in. I took off my clothes and sank down into the steaming bubbles. It was an awkward situation, this disappearance of Sherlock's. It looked bizarre.

"Joel?" said Marilyn outside the door. "Are you thinking? Or are you just dreaming in there?"

"I'm thinking," I said. "Don't worry. I'm thinking."

I sank lower into the bubbles, until they were brushing my chin, but still nothing came to mind. Because how many ways were there for a large dog to disappear from a hotel suite?

"Are you still in the tub, Joel?" said Marilyn. "Are you concentrating?"

"For God's sake!" I yelled. "Yes! I'm concentrating! Just leave me alone."

"There is no reason for you to be *rude*," said Marilyn. And then there was silence.

I was beginning to wonder how JJ could ever have fallen in love with Marilyn Schumacher. When she became excited her voice went up very high, at least an octave. And, in pajamas with elephants on them, and smeared mascara, and little bags under her eyes, she did not look too alluring. She looked just like anybody else.

"Joel?" said Marilyn softly. "Are you still there?"

"No," I said, "I'm not. I drowned."

"Don't be silly, Joel. . . . Have you come up with anything?"

"No."

"Do you want me to come in and scrub your back for you?"

"No, Marilyn! Of course not."

"Well, I was just *asking*, Joel. I thought it might relax you. I mean, we have to come up with an idea."

But we didn't, and a half hour later, as the two of us sat on the couch watching television I felt very nervous. Solly and Mike had been gone for over an hour. Ominously, we heard their key turning in the lock.

"Breakfast time!" said Solly, as he bustled into the room. "Straight from McDonald's. Pancakes, scrambled eggs, bacon, toast, and juice. Nothin' but the best."

"You should see the traffic down on Fourteenth Street," said Mike. "A disaster."

With a sinking heart, I thought of Sherlock. Was he dead by now, or—by some miracle—was he trotting up Fifth Avenue towards Eighty-second Street? In my mind's eye I saw him passing the Public Library and heading towards Rockefeller Center. Then passing the Plaza Hotel and the Pierre. Would anyone notice him, trotting along that way? Would he be able to dodge the traffic?

Solly cleared the coffee table and spread out our breakfast. He turned the television to channel 4 and dug into his food. Mike did the same. They did not seem to notice Sherlock's absence.

"Best eggs I've had in a long time," Solly said to

me. "Moist, but not too moist. You can't beat Mc-Donald's."

"Yeah," said Mike, wiping butter off his chin. "For the price, the food is good. You can't beat it."

I looked at Marilyn and she looked at me. She shrugged.

"Solly and me, we stopped for a shave at Leo's Barbershop," said Mike. "That's why we took so long."

"Yeah," said Solly. "We chewed the fat a little. We *schmoozed*."

"Anyone hear the weather report today?" asked Mike. "It's gonna rain or what? It's gonna be cloudy?"

And then Solly said, "Hey. Where's the dog?"

"The dog?" I said politely.

"Yeah. That big dog. Where is he?"

"Uh, I don't know," I replied. "Marilyn, have you seen the dog?"

Marilyn swallowed hard. "No, Joel. Not lately."

Solly was on his feet now, looking around the room. "Jesus," he said, "where's the dog? A dog just doesn't vanish. What did you do with him?"

"I didn't do *anything* with him," I said coldly.

"The last I saw, he was sleeping in Marilyn's bed-room."

Solly went into Marilyn's bedroom and came out again. "There ain't no dog in there. He's gone."

"How could he be gone?" I asked. "You locked us in here. All three of us."

"Beats me," said Solly, scratching his head.

Mike was on his hands and knees, looking under the furniture. "He's gone," he said. "That big dog is gone."

"Well," I sighed, "that's life. Win some, lose some."

"Don't you *care*?" said Solly. "Your dog disappears and you don't care?"

"Yeah," said Mike. "You don't care? What's the matter with you?"

"He was a very nice dog," said Solly. "What did you call him? Sherlock?"

"That's right."

"So where is he?" said Mike.

"Beats me," I said.

This conversation might have gone on for a long time—hours, perhaps—except for the fact that just at that moment, the door to our hotel suite was kicked in. Nobody knocked, nobody pounded, they just kicked in the door. And there before my eyes were JJ, my father, two policemen, and Mr. Schumacher.

Suddenly, things got very lively. Marilyn rushed into JJ's arms and began to cry. The policemen arrested Solly and Mike. My father hugged me, and Mr. Schumacher just stood there looking stunned. Then Solly and Mike's brother-in-law, who owns the hotel, came upstairs to see what all the commotion was—and then his wife, who owns the beauty parlor, appeared and tried to calm everyone down. It was a real madhouse, and comical in a way, but all I could think of was Sherlock.

I pulled my father into the hallway. "I can't believe that he made it!" I said. "Sherlock, I mean. It was over sixty blocks."

"What are you talking about?" said my father. He looked haggard and he needed a shave.

"Sherlock! Didn't he get home all right? Didn't you read the note?"

"He got home all right," said my father, "but not on foot. Is that what you thought?"

"Marilyn and I lowered him out of the window.

We told him to go home."

"Joel," said my father, "Sherlock came home in a cab. Some woman found him wandering around Fourteenth Street, read his name and address on his dog tag, and gave a cabbie money to bring him home. One of the doormen brought him up in the elevator, and when Hannah took off his collar she found the note. Sherlock was exhausted. He went straight to your room and fell asleep."

"God," I said. "But is he all right?"

"He's in better shape than the rest of us," said my father tiredly. "Come on, Joel. Let's go home."

11

DURING THE NEXT few days, a great many things came to light. First of all, Marilyn and I discovered why Mr. Schumacher wouldn't pay the ransom. My father had been right in the first place—Schumacher was involved in a defense project in Washington and thought he was being blackmailed. Secondly, Marilyn discovered—to her amazement—that Mrs. Hornblow, to whom she owed the fifty thousand, didn't really expect it to be paid. I mean, the ladies who had been playing bridge that day were all a little drunk, on white wine, which is why the stakes got so high. Mrs. Hornblow was horrified to learn that Marilyn had taken the gambling debt seriously. So much for fifty thousand.

As for Solly and Mike, Marilyn refused to press charges against them—telling me that she had gotten fond of them and didn't want to see them in jail. *Fond* is not the way *I* felt about Solly and Mike, but to each his own. They returned to their dry cleaning business—but whether or not they ever went to Florida, I don't know.

The interesting thing is that JJ and Marilyn got back together again—only this time around, it was different. Marilyn agreed to go into therapy, to see why she had such a strong need to seduce every man she met—and JJ enrolled at The New School, in the writing program. Considering his success with *Stirring Constantly*, I thought this was a very humble thing to do. But he had writer's block now, he told me, and needed to go back to basics.

Was Mr. Schumacher angry about the whole thing? Yes. He was furious. But on the other hand, he was so relieved to have Marilyn back that he tried to be understanding with her. The only thing he asked was that she give up bridge.

All of which brings the story around to me, Joel.

It's funny how much praise I received after the kidnapping—for using my head and sending Sherlock home, for trying so hard to find Marilyn—but the odd thing was that the more my parents praised me, the quieter I became. It was like I didn't need their praise anymore. Or, at least, not as much as I used to.

"The whole thing was very intelligent," Hannah said to me as we sat at the kitchen table together. "The way you organized it all. You must have been holding many good thoughts, to find Marilyn that way."

"Well . . ." I began.

"You keep on holding those thoughts and you will *be* somebody one day, Joel Greenberg. You will turn into a senator or a lawyer or a TV anchorman. Something like that."

"You really think so?" I asked Hannah. I was eating a piece of her devil's food cake.

"No doubt about it, Joel. Because you are a person who uses his *head*. It is crystal clear to everyone."

One more thing about Marilyn. She started working with me in the Park soon after that—helping the homeless people, handing out food. It was like our experience together had forged a new bond between us. Or maybe she was just grateful to me for rescuing her. At any rate, she and I hand out food together three times a week now, near the Metropolitan Museum. Marilyn is even thinking of doing some work at Safety House, downtown, where they help runaway kids.

She's a pretty good person after all. Marilyn Schumacher.